Charles Buchan's
SPURS
GIFT BOOK

selections from
CHARLES BUCHAN'S PUBLICATIONS
1951-73

Dear Reader,

As this is the first Gift Book which I have edited for you, I would like to begin this little introduction by saying how much I hope you will enjoy the stories and pictures which have been gathered together for you.

I expect many of you who are reading this are already old friends of mine, boys who keep in touch with our greatest game through the columns of "Football Monthly". But, whether we have already met, or whether we are meeting here for the first time, I welcome you all, knowing how keen you are on sport and how sound is your judgement.

Now it is your judgement that can help me. Let me know if you enjoy this book - and if you do like it, tell your pals about it.

If, on the other hand, you have criticisms to make, let me know of them and you can be sure I will do my very best to carry out your suggestions when we publish this book in future years.

The idea has been to give you variety, to provide exciting reading, and to print pictures which will capture highlights of the game and the great footballers who make it so popular with us all.

I believe the recipe will be to your liking and hope that when you have finished this volume you will begin to look forward to next year's!

**Charles Buchan's introduction
to his first Soccer Gift Book, 1953–1954**

Charles Buchan's Spurs Gift Book
© Malavan Media and Football Monthly Ltd 2008

Malavan Media is a creative consultancy responsible for the
Played in Britain series of books and events
www.playedinbritain.co.uk

Edited by Simon Inglis
Text by Julie Welch and Simon Inglis
Design by Doug Cheeseman
Production by Jackie Spreckley
Thanks to Simon Gill and Theo Inglis
ISBN: 978 0954744571
Printed by Zrinski, Croatia

Charles Buchan's
SPURS
GIFT BOOK

Edited by
Simon Inglis

Introduction by
Julie Welch

Published by Malavan Media

Con

ents

TALKING IT OVER... by JOHN THOMPSON

From the beginning...

AT first there was one chair in the office of "Football Monthly." I cannot remember why. We were hard-up for furniture for a long time. We would take it in turns to perch round a trestle table on orange boxes and would courteously leave the chair for any visitor who proved himself healthy enough to climb the steep stairs leading to our new home.

The trestle table was covered with a grey blanket and smelled of old apples. This was probably because Covent Garden was just round the corner.

Long before "Football Monthly" increased its tangible assets in any substantial way, Charles Buchan climbed the stairs with a purchase wrapped in brown paper. **It was a splendidly expensive feather-duster.**

Every morning Charles would whisk it energetically over the walls, the little pieces of furniture and the weary strips of linoleum.

Then he would look around as proudly as if he had just scored the winning goal against Scotland.

The moment he had finished, all the dust would settle down gracefully to await the next disturbance. The office overlooked the Strand, London . . . buses almost passed through the room, and it was difficult to keep clean for any time at all.

That first winter was singularly comfortless. In an unenviable spot, furthest from the windows, Joe Sarl would peer with a kind of hopeless determination at typescript and proofs and emerge at the end of the day with the lost look of a man who has been wandering through a thick fog.

He was, however, the warmest of our company.

To avoid frost-bite from the draughts that whistled through the room, Charles Buchan would wrap newspapers round his legs. The paper rustled disconcertingly whenever he moved.

LONG before winter fell, there had been the task of reading the first contributions to our first issue. There had been a fascinating incongruity in sitting on an orange box and studying the earliest article to arrive.

It came from that fine and kindly friend, the Marquess of Londonderry. He had been converted to Soccer by his friendship with miners in his father's pits.

There was a certain dream-like quality in reading Lord Londonderry's description of how he had become a director of Arsenal . . . because of a conversation over dinner at Buckingham Palace with the Master of the Horse, who happened to be Chairman of Arsenal.

Well, Buckingham Palace was only down the road from our office. And for a moment the bare electric light bulb was a candelabrum . . .

As this one hundredth edition of "Football Monthly" was being prepared, I glanced with nostalgia through that long-ago Number One.

The front cover picture was of Stanley Matthews, of Blackpool and England. **There could be no other choice, for Matthews has enriched the pleasures of us all and, in the years that have intervened, there has been no challenger for his place among the giants.**

Inside, were pictures of little Henry Cockburn, of Manchester United, and of Jimmy Dickinson, who has served Portsmouth with devoted loyalty through so many triumphs and disasters.

There, too, were bow-legged Joe Mercer and Mal Griffiths, the happy Welshman, and George Young leading out Scotland, and Jimmy Mason poised over the ball in the colours of Third Lanark. All were players remembered now with gratitude.

There, too, was Joe Harvey, telling with humility of the day Newcastle United won the F.A. Cup . . . *The King handed it to me and as he did so, I had the feeling that all the good people of Tyneside were with me . . . I felt that His Majesty was giving the Cup to me not as Joe Harvey, but as the representative of all those supporters, that I was getting it on their behalf.*

The Queen gave me my medal and I made my way down the steps, perhaps stumbling a little because I was near to tears . . .

TURN again the yellowing pages of that old "Football Monthly". Here is Raich Carter talking of bomb-battered Hull . . . *It was the success of Hull City Soccer team that helped to put Hull back on the map and restore the morale of people who had come to regard themselves as isolated and forgotten . . .*

Arthur Drewry, then Chairman of England's Selectors, told how *his imagination had been fired in Argentina and Brazil by the development of football grounds as first-class social centres; the centre-piece of the local community for every kind of recreative sport . . .*

Turn the pages . . . here is J. B. Priestley, capturing, as he did so well in "The Good Companions", the emotions of those who follow our greatest game . . . *It turned you into a member of a new community, all brothers together for an hour-and-a-half, for not only had you escaped from the clanking machinery of this less life, from work, wages, rent, doles, sick pay, insurance cards, nagging wives, ailing children, bad bosses, idle workmen, but you had escaped with most of your neighbours, with half the town, and there you were, cheering together, thumping one another on the shoulders, swopping judgments like lords of the earth, having pushed your way through a turnstile into another and altogether more splendid kind of life, hurtling with Conflict and yet passionate and beautiful in its Art . . .*

AND now, close the pages and consider for a moment how "Football Monthly" grew from its orange-box days into the voice of the greatest game man ever played, the game that spans frontiers with a handshake and knows no barriers of race or belief.

"Football Monthly" became a unique 'family affair'. Readers sent ideas and views on how to improve the magazine. Never had a publication received such friendly and loyal support.

The family was scattered, as the magic of football is scattered.

There was a boy in Brazil, a shoe-maker in Alaska, a judge's son in Yugoslavia, the skipper of a tug-boat who took two copies so that he could send one to an unknown kid in hospital.

There was a cinema manager in Australia, a cipher clerk in a British Embassy, a lance-corporal in the Malayan jungle.

The addresses from which they wrote ranged from Bolton to Burma. They came from destroyers and trawlers, factories and farms. Some were from village schools, others at Eton.

Thus did "Football Monthly" prosper because of the kindliness and understanding of its readers.

And it is the kindliness that will be remembered always— the gifts that readers asked us to send to sick children at Christmas, the gestures that helped old players down on their luck.

There were letters from prisons and mansions and there was the miracle of finding how blind people retain their love for football.

And the family grew and gained in strength and influence. It is loyal and sturdy, as it always was. We are very proud of it . . .

▲ December 1959

Foreword

by **Simon Inglis**
Played in Britain series editor

'Our object is to provide a publication that will be worthy of our National game and the grand sportsmen who play and watch it.'

For the discerning football fan of the 1950s and 1960s, *Charles Buchan's Football Monthly* was an absolute essential. If not for reading, then for the supply of bedroom posters.

Of course there were other publications on the market, such as the weekly *Sport* magazine, which ran until 1957, or *Soccer Star*, established in 1952. But neither had such bold design, such vibrant colour images, the collectability, the satisfying weightiness, nor any of the camaraderie that Charles Buchan and his team so knowingly infused into the pages of *Football Monthly*.

To be a reader of Charlie's magazine was to be a member of a fraternity.

In the world of Charles Buchan – a former Sunderland and Arsenal player known to millions for his match reports on BBC Radio – football was Soccer (always with a capital S), and Soccer was 'grand'. Indeed most things in Charlie's world were grand. The players were grand, the matches were grand, the footballing life itself was grand.

Buchan's magazine first appeared in September 1951 (when Charlie was already aged 61), just as the Festival of Britain was winding down on London's South Bank. Rationing was still in place. Paper was still in short supply. National Service was still obligatory for young men, while thousands of British troops were serving in Korea.

In the six years since Hitler's defeat, attendance levels at English football had soared to record levels, topping 41 million in 1948–49. Yet never before had the fortunes of the national team been so low, following England's humiliating defeat by the USA during the 1950 World Cup in Brazil (a match witnessed by Buchan and several of the Fleet Street veterans who would become his regular contributors).

Thus hope for the future, in the bright new world of post-war Britain, was necessarily tempered by anxiety concerning the health of the national game. Similarly, parochial pride in our footballing greats had always to be counterbalanced by reluctant admiration for the obvious skills of those 'Continentals' and 'Latins' from overseas. Hot-headed and devious they may have been, but clearly they had much to teach us, about tactics, training, even what kind of boots to wear.

So successful was *Charles Buchan's Football Monthly* that in July 1953 the publishers issued the first *Charles Buchan's Soccer Gift Book*. For the next two decades this jaunty annual earned an automatic slot on the Christmas wish lists of thousands of schoolboys.

Buchan himself, despite his reporting commitments with the BBC and the *News Chronicle* – whose staff he had joined in 1928 after retiring from Arsenal – remained actively involved in both publications until his death in June 1960, while on holiday in Monte Carlo. He was a tall man, always immaculately dressed and unfailingly polite. Columnist John Macadam, another writer of the old school, said of him, 'Charles sees only the good in all men.' But whereas Macadam and several of his fellow writers were hard drinking adventurers, Buchan retained the image of a schoolmasterly gent. And yet in his prime he had been both a supremely gifted and wily inside forward – his ratio of 224 goals in 413 games for Sunderland still stands as a record – and a brave soldier, winning a Military Cross during the First World War (a fact he modestly omitted from his autobiography, published in 1955).

By 1958 *Football Monthly's* circulation had risen to 107,000, at which point the offices moved from the Strand to 161-166 Fleet Street.

By a curious coincidence, this was the site of Andertons Hotel, where the Football League had formed in 1888. Not only that but the new building, Hulton House, was owned by the former publishers of *Athletic News*, once Britain's most popular football weekly.

After Charlie's death the proprietors kept his name on the masthead (until 1971), and under new editor Pat Collins – buoyed up by England's World Cup victory in 1966 – increased circulation to 200,000 in 1968. The following year it reached an all-time peak of 254,000. Membership of the Boys' Club topped 100,000.

Changing fashions may explain part of the magazine's demise in the early 1970s. As hairstyles lengthened and trousers grew more flared, more young readers were veering away from programme and autograph swaps in favour of records and pop-related memorabilia. Football itself was entering a period of decline, as the ravages of hooliganism began to take their toll on attendances.

Charlie's seemingly more innocent world was fading rapidly.

But also crucial was the decision by *Football Monthly's* new holding company, Longacre Press, to publish a sister magazine called *Goal*, in 1968. It took two years for *Goal* to outsell *Football Monthly*. Then a third contender materialised in the form of *Shoot*, a brash new weekly, published by IPC.

Shoot and *Goal* each sold over 220,000 copies weekly in 1971, compared with 164,000, and falling, for *Football Monthly*.

In August 1973 the publishers responded by rebranding the title in a smaller format. But as editor Pat Collins suspected, it was a losing battle, and in August 1974 the title left Fleet Street and became *Football Magazine*.

A golden era had truly passed.

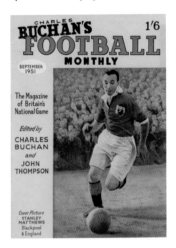

The compilation which follows is selected from issues of *Charles Buchan's Football Monthly* dating 1951–73, and from the *Charles Buchan's Soccer Gift Books*, published annually from 1953–74.

Inevitably readers will spot gaps; star players unmentioned, key events uncovered. Some of these omissions arise from lack of space. Others are simply owing to the fact that the magazine and gift books were by no means comprehensive in their coverage. If there is a narrative in what follows, therefore, it is fractured rather than cohesive, though hopefully no less appealing when viewed as a whole.

It will be noted that this book forms part of *Played in Britain*, a series which seeks to celebrate and preserve these islands' extraordinary sporting heritage.

Heritage is generally thought to reside in historic buildings, in places and landscapes. What it is hoped the following pages demonstrate is that there is heritage in ephemera too, and in the shared narrative that make us a nation, and a footballing nation at that.

For more on the Charles Buchan archive, see our list of related publications on the back page.

Charles Buchan's

ALBUM OF ACTION

Something to shout about. Ted Ditchburn makes a flying save in the match between Tottenham Hotspur and Newcastle United. Spurs won by 3-1.

Spurs 1951-73

by Julie Welch

Those pictures of the 1961 Double win are hard-wired into our minds: the crowd streaming across the pitch at the final whistle, chanting, 'We want Danny, We want Danny', after victory against Sheffield Wednesday clinched the title; the team climbing up to the Royal Box to collect their FA Cup winners' medals; the open top bus parade through the streets of Tottenham a day later; Danny Blanchflower raising the Championship trophy on high at a packed White Hart Lane after the final home game of the season.

Together, these are images of triumph and perfection that forever established Tottenham Hotspur's reputation around the world – and ensured that I, for one, could never countenance supporting any other football club.

I was eleven when I discovered the fabulous Spurs in 1959. I had just started at a new school with a catchment area that covered vast swathes of North London, and my three best friends came from families who were Tottenham fans through and through.

The club seemed glamorous and sophisticated, with a team of brilliant, good-looking heroes. Other girls in our class had photos of Cliff or Elvis sellotaped to the underside of their desk lids. We had Blanchflower, Mackay and White.

I had no interest in Tottenham's past, only their amazing present. The start of the 1950s seemed like prehistory to me, and it was not until adulthood that I realised Bill Nicholson's Double-winning side were not the first from White Hart Lane to achieve enduring greatness.

Exactly a decade earlier, another Spurs team had already reached that pinnacle.

By the end of the 1950-1951 season, a few months before the first edition of *Charles Buchan's Football Monthly* went on sale in September 1951, Tottenham were already attracting attention as the most exciting club in England.

After more than a decade of drabness and disruption caused by the war, fans at White Hart Lane found themselves treated to some spellbinding performances, as manager Arthur Rowe's visionary methods steered Spurs to the Second Division title in 1950, followed twelve, scarcely believable months later, by the League championship.

Those seasons, and especially the name of Rowe, would forever be linked with a style of football that is still recognised today, 'push and run'.

Tottenham born and raised, during the 1930s Rowe had played as an attacking centre-half for Spurs (his only club as a professional), before beginning his managerial career at Chelmsford City in 1945.

At this time Spurs were in the Second Division, having been relegated in 1935. Rowe's appointment in May 1949 was therefore a considerable gamble. Any longer in the lower division and they risked becoming middling also-rans.

Yet Rowe's impact was almost immediate. Keeping possession through quick, accurate passes and transferring the ball from man to man in as short a route as possible to goal, with no elaborate ball play and little or no dribbling, Rowe's 'push and run' formula put the onus relentlessly on forward movement.

For three seasons, from 1949 to 1952, Spurs in full cry represented one of the most thrilling sights in football. 'Even when goalkeeper Ted Ditchburn holds the ball in his arms, Spurs are attacking.' That was how Tottenham's style was summed up in the first ever issue of *Football Monthly*.

But this success was not simply a matter of playing a system.

Rowe had assembled a squad of players who possessed the finest skills of the game. 'Worth a king's ransom in transfer fees', as a later *Football Monthly* article put it, even though Rowe actually made only one major signing, full back Alf Ramsey from Southampton, for £21,000.

It was from the 'push and run' era that Spurs derived their reputation not only as a glamour club, but also one with an attitude that winning was not enough in itself. As that September 1951 article concluded, 'Spurs are undoubtedly the pattern on which other League clubs have moulded their styles. Their fast movements have also brought back some of the old spectacular appeal to the game, and they have set a fashion that must lead to a big improvement in the general standard of League football.'

West Ham had their academy. Manchester United had their youth policy. But Spurs were the club that always had to win well.

Their glittering line-up of stars figured strongly in the magazine during the early 1950s, among them Ted Ditchburn, Harry Clarke ('effectively closing the midfield like a second edition of Leslie Compton at his best') and George Robb.

Up front was the big, magnificent Channel Islander, Len Duquemin, whose 'deft flicks and a habit of taking the opposing centre-half out of position have led to many Spurs goals.'

Then there was the crowd's favourite, Eddie Baily, who, in John Thompson's words, had 'a wonderful exuberance about his play which lights up the dullest day. His coolness often amounts to impudence and to London crowds he is probably the most popular of all London footballers'.

Bill Nicholson, the right half during this period, will of course always be indelibly identified with Spurs – a man who devoted his life to the club as player, coach, manager, chief scout and president.

But in amongst that talent, the one player who really stood out was the Welshman, Ron Burgess.

Burgess, wrote Julian Holland in *The Double,* published in 1961, was 'a conquistador, faultless in technique, tireless in energy, matchless in skill, ceaseless in ardour, one of the great left-halves of all time'.

Bill Nicholson agreed. As Cliff Jones later commented, Nicholson considered Burgess 'the best wing half Tottenham ever had'.

Strangely, another great player from that side is often overlooked when it comes to assessing who are the greatest Spurs of all time.

Because his name is synonymous with England and the World Cup, it is easy to forget what the cool, cultured Alf Ramsey – 'captain and general of the side' – meant to Tottenham in the immediate post-war era. In this respect, John Thompson's feature on Ramsey in January 1952, calling him 'The Five Elms "General"', was truly prescient.

Ramsey 'sees the game not only as it affects his own local duties, but as a complete design in which defence and attack and right and left are fluid and must flow together... He owes much to the guidance he has received from manager Arthur Rowe and is grateful for it.'

Inevitably, the impact of 'push and run' soon wore off. After finishing second to Manchester United in the league in 1952, the team had to settle for no more than a Cup semi-final place in 1953.

That April, *Football Monthly's* 'Spotlight on Tottenham Hotspur' observed tactfully, 'It may be that Tottenham have not carried all before them this season. That is because they had a strenuous tour in Canada and the United States last summer, and they are feeling the after effects.'

But there was more to it than that. 'Push and run' had succeeded because it was innovative and took opponents completely by surprise. Also, it was hugely demanding. For it to work players had to be at the very top of their game. Once they lost their edge, form or fitness, the system failed.

So it was that with other clubs working out at last how to beat them, Spurs found themselves near the foot of the table by late 1953.

Clearly, Rowe had to rebuild. But that, too, did not work out as planned. Several reserve players did not make the grade, while a delve into the transfer market failed to unearth any with the necessary talent and dynamism. The tale of the next two years was therefore one of decline, much of it due to Rowe's excessive loyalty to the title winners of 1951.

Although it was the old guard who took Spurs to the last eight of the Cup in 1954, their 3-0 defeat by West Bromwich Albion signalled the end of an era.

Rowe took the break-up of his ageing team so much to heart that his health was affected seriously enough to land him in hospital.

Reading between the lines, the story of Spurs now being told in *Football Monthly* was that of a side whose glory days were behind them. Ronnie Burgess admitted in the *1954–55 Gift Book*, 'Until two or three seasons ago I was recognised as an attacking wing-half-back. This has always been my natural game, but Father Time has a habit of taking his toll of one's physical strength... That's why my attacking bent had to be curbed, and my all-out dashes into the opposition goalmouth made less frequently.'

Particularly poignant was the photo in April 1954 of a frail-looking Rowe at the door of the dressing room, patting Burgess on the shoulder as the team headed out to the pitch. 'Even during his long illness this season, the respect which Tottenham Hotspur players feel for manager Arthur Rowe has inspired them to put all they know into their games...'

It was not enough. Spurs' shock defeat by Third Division York in the FA Cup Fifth Round in February 1955 was the last straw. After a second breakdown, Rowe handed over the reins to long-serving trainer Jimmy Anderson.

Rowe never returned to White Hart Lane again.

Yet his attempts to rebuild Spurs had not been completely fruitless. Not long before bowing out, Rowe made a crucial signing.

Danny Blanchflower's £30,000 move from Aston Villa made the Northern Irishman the most expensive midfielder in Britain. But the price was immaterial.

Blanchflower was just the charismatic, proven leader needed to galvanise the side. The big question was, at the age of 29, how many seasons did he have left?

There was no need to worry. Danny Blanchflower was to achieve more with Spurs in the next ten years than many players would in an entire lifetime. Eloquent, independent-minded and witty, Blanchflower was a complete original, as well as an outstanding talent. He read the game expertly, was a master of distribution and a natural tactician. In the words of Julian Holland, 'Here was a footballing genius who could match the great Burgess both as player and captain, and yet bring to the game the detached thinking and intellect of a Rowe.'

For journalists, Blanchflower was compellingly quotable.

'The game is about glory. It is about doing things in style and with a flourish, about going out and beating the other lot, not waiting for them to die of boredom.'

Such was Blanchflower's philosophy. To Scotty Hall, in the October 1957 *Football Monthly*, he offered the *aperçu*, 'What's the point of saying something you don't believe? Might as well keep your mouth shut.'

Then there was the time at Barnsley, his first English club, when he complained to manager Angus Seed about the lack of ball-practice in training.

'If you don't see the ball during the week,' said Seed, 'you'll be more keen to get it on Saturdays.'

'But if I don't get some practice,' retorted Blanchflower, 'I won't know what to do with it when I do get it on Saturdays.'

Happily for Spurs, Blanchflower's arrival coincided with a return to form for Tommy Harmer, portrayed in the *1957-58 Gift Book* as balanced and as graceful as a prototype Ronaldo.

During the Rowe years, this unparalleled juggler and outrageous dummier had been unable to hold down a regular place in a team encouraged not to hold onto the ball. Jimmy Anderson not only found Harmer a regular niche but made him the key front line man.

The White Hart Lane cheque book now came into frequent use as Anderson worked on rebuilding the side. One important signing was country boy Maurice Norman, memorably described by Ivan Ponting (see Links) as 'cantering down the centre of the pitch with neck outstretched and long limbs extended in unexpected directions, like some fantastic cross between a runaway giraffe and a quick-stepping spider.'

Across town from Chelsea came the mighty goal-scorer Bobby

Smith, destined, like Norman, to achieve legendary status with the Double side. They were swiftly followed by Welsh international winger Terry Medwin, to fill the vacancy left by Sonny Walters.

In 1957 Medwin was followed to White Hart Lane by his Wales and former Swansea Town colleague Cliff Jones, at £35,000 the most expensive footballer in Britain and destined within a few years to be regarded as one of the greatest wingers in the world.

Meanwhile, Edmonton boy Tony Marchi broke into the first team and proved to be such an influential player that, capitalising on his Italian ancestry, Juventus whisked him off to Turin for an astonishing £42,000. Other future stars like Ron Henry, Peter Baker and Terry Dyson were also developing well.

Things never quite gelled under Anderson, though. In particular Danny Blanchflower's habit of making tactical decisions on the pitch did not go down well with his manager. After Blanchflower sent Maurice Norman up front to help the hunt for an equaliser during Spurs' FA Cup semi-final against Manchester City in March 1956 – a switch that proved fruitless – Anderson stripped him of the captaincy and dropped him for a vital relegation match against Cardiff. Typically, when contacted by the press, Blanchflower refused to play along with the official pretence that he was injured and made it clear he had been dropped.

Still, by the end of 1957–58, Spurs looked as if they might be going places again. Certainly the season closed in personal triumph for Blanchflower, who led them out of the early season doldrums to a third place finish in the League.

He also won the Footballer of the Year Award and in the summer played for Northern Ireland in the World Cup in Sweden.

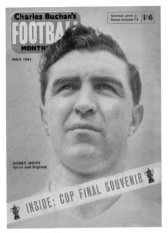

▲ May 1961

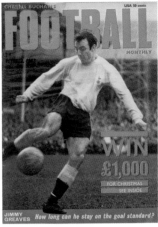

▲ October 1967

They made it to the quarter finals, unlike England.

On the 'plane home, outspoken as always, Blanchflower sat next to Joe Mercer and Stan Cullis and told them that he believed the Double could be done. Not only that, he said, Spurs were the side to do it.

Such a prediction soon looked impossibly optimistic. In the opening weeks of 1958–59 season, Spurs amassed just three points in seven games, conceding 19 goals in the process. As his team plummeted down the table, Jimmy Anderson resigned.

In his place, in October 1958, the board promoted head coach Bill Nicholson. The man who had spent most of his playing days in Alf Ramsey's shadow was now most definitely in charge.

Nicholson's first game gave a vivid glimpse of what was to come as Spurs thrashed Everton 10-4.

'We don't score ten every week,' Tommy Harmer warned the new boss as the players left the pitch to a standing ovation. But typically, Nicholson was more concerned about the defence. In his first four games it leaked 15 goals.

The trouble lay at wing-half, where both Blanchflower and Jim Iley were attack-minded players who left enormous gaps in front of the full backs as they motored forward. By the end of the year, Spurs had won just once in eleven matches, forcing Nicholson to drop Blanchflower to make way for a more defensive-minded wing half.

Reshuffled, Spurs now won four games in a row, while Blanchflower, worried that he only had a few years left at the top, asked for a transfer. Nicholson told him frankly that he would put his request before the board, but would strongly recommend their turning it down. In the position they were in, Spurs could not afford to lose him. 'But,' said Nicholson, 'later on if you still

want to go, we'll reconsider it.'

As Nicholson had warned, the board duly refused to let him go, and Blanchflower's request was never mentioned again. For as the weeks wore on it became obvious that Spurs were nothing without his creative flair. As a result, restored to the team and to the captaincy, Blanchflower was effectively handed *carte blanche* to run the show on the pitch.

Immediately Spurs pulled away from the relegation zone, and from that moment on there appeared to be no stopping the new Spurs.

A combination of Nicholson's genius for team-building and Spurs' spending power brought what was arguably the most crucial purchase, when, for £32,000 – the highest fee ever paid in Britain for a half-back – Dave Mackay signed twelve hours before the March 1959 transfer deadline.

Scottish fans knew all about Dave Mackay. Captain of Hearts since the age of 22, he had won all the honours going in his home country, earning a reputation as a forceful, if not brutal, tackler. Opponents and managers alike complained, to the extent that at one stage the Scottish selectors were urged to drop him.

Profiled in *Football Monthly* in December 1959, the Edinburgh man, only 5 feet 7 inches in height but with the presence of a giant, was quick to defend himself.

'I know my tackling has been criticised, but I insist that I am a fair, if strong, tackler. I have always played that way, for I believe that the main job of a wing-half is to GET the ball.'

But Mackay was not just a ball-winning enforcer. He was an exceptionally skilled player as well. He and Blanchflower might have been completely different personalities, but their admiration was mutual. As Julian Holland wrote, 'The understanding that

developed between these two giants was immediate: Mackay seemed to interpret Blanchflower as though they had played together as boys or, in a previous life, on some wild Celtic field...'

Alan Mullery, who took over Blanchflower's role later on in the 1960s, put it more simply: They were 'the perfect wing-half combination who combined power, flair and mutual understanding.'

Mackay was not the only player lured from Scotland. For a mere £16,500 Dundee's Bill Brown became Spurs' goalkeeper in June 1959. In October he was joined by Falkirk's John White, seemingly frail but with skills that would see him establish his place in arguably the greatest Spurs midfield ever.

When Les Allen signed from Chelsea in December 1959 to join Smith and Dyson in the forward line, the assembly of the Double side was complete.

For *Football Monthly*, Spurs were once again a regular source of stories. In April 1961 it reproduced a photo of Blanchflower rooted to the spot, as a goal from Jimmy Walsh of Leicester City stripped Spurs of their unbeaten home record. This was just weeks after Blanchflower's most celebrated show of independence when he had responded to Eamonn Andrews' invitation to appear on ITV's *This Is Your Life* with the memorable, 'Oh no, it isn't!'

As *Football Monthly's* wry photo caption reminded Blanchflower, 'THIS is your life, Danny!'

Meanwhile, in the same edition, 'Salad Days At White Hart Lane' reported, 'England's top club team of the year have packed in the fans, home and away, as no post-war side has done – not even Manchester United in their pre-Munich glory days.'

Football Monthly celebrated The Double itself twice, on the June

1961 cover, and in the July issue, with Blanchflower seen leading the 'Team of the Century' down the steps from the Royal Box after the FA Cup win over Leicester.

Later on in 1961, Spurs took on Europe. November's *Football Monthly* recorded a remarkable comeback against Gornik, a team of Polish part-timers who had thrashed Spurs 4-2 in the away leg in Katowice.

Cliff Jones remembers the White Hart Lane return match to this day. 'When we came on to the pitch, the atmosphere was indescribable. The crowd was right on top of you, unlike at European stadiums where there was running track, with the crowd 10 to 15 yards back. Gornik were intimidated. The supporters just picked that up, and we tore into Gornik. They never stood a chance. We beat them 8-1. White Hart Lane was a very, very, special place.'

Not that Nicholson rested on his laurels. Three months after that European victory he brought to White Hart Lane a player who was to break goalkeepers' spirits for several seasons to come and, in the process, alongside Denis Law become the most frequently featured player on *Football Monthly's* pages during the 1960s.

Signed from Milan for the famous sum of £99,999, Jimmy Greaves crowned his first appearance at the Lane by delivering a hat-trick in Spurs' 5-2 thrashing of Blackpool.

So while John White was cover boy for September 1962, inside the magazine it was the size of Greaves' transfer fee and his eye-watering wages that reinforced Tottenham's image as England's most wealthy, glamorous club.

In January 1963, a photo feature compared scenes of 'ultrasophisticated' White Hart Lane – 'football in the £100-a-week, Jaguar class' – with the vast expanse of Hackney Marshes. ▶

'Whether at Tottenham or Old Trafford, in street, on waste land or marsh – the spirit of this great game is the same,' reckoned the caption.

Perhaps on the pitch, but off it, there could be no denying that the abolition of the maximum wage in 1961 had already begun the process whereby top footballers became increasingly distanced from the working men on the terraces.

Greaves went on to score 21 goals in 22 League appearances that season, almost enough for Spurs to clinch the title for the second year in succession. A defeat, ironically by Alf Ramsey's Ipswich, ended that hope, but *Football Monthly's* photo spread in July 1962 showed the FA Cup victory against Burnley, a win that sent Spurs back into Europe.

The following season Greaves did even better, scoring 37 goals, a new club record. Spurs also made history by becoming the first British team to win European honours.

'Glory, glory hallelujah!' read the *Football Monthly* caption in July 1963, after Spurs' stunning 5-1 defeat of Atletico Madrid in the European Cup Winners' Cup final in Rotterdam. Said Man of the Match Terry Dyson, 'It's the first time I can remember when Bill had no negative thoughts or criticism after a game. It was almost as if that was the absolute peak performance for his team, the one that he had been working towards... Bill was absolutely ecstatic.'

With good reason. Atletico, one of the great Continental sides of the day, had been annihilated in what it is still regarded as one of the greatest performances by any English team in Europe.

Yet just as the 'push and run' side of the early 1950s had faded ten years before, that glorious night in Rotterdam might also be seen as the pinnacle for the Double side. Seven months later, in December

1963, Dave Mackay broke his leg at Old Trafford in a second round Cup Winners' Cup tie against Manchester United. In April 1964 Danny Blanchflower finally bowed to the inevitable and left to pursue a career in journalism. Bobby Smith, slower and heavier now, was sold to Brighton. Terry Medwin sustained a broken leg on a tour of South Africa.

But all these misfortunes were as nothing compared to what happened that July.

Struck down by lightning at Crews Hill golf course, Enfield, John White's tragic death caused unimaginable grief to his 22-year-old widow, Sandra, a two year old daughter and a baby son.

For the club and his team-mates, the blow was devastating too.

'Football can ill afford to lose men like John White. Players of his skill and intelligence are rare...' as a Star Strip tribute in the *1967-68 Gift Book* later put it.

Only weeks before his death, Bill Nicholson had apparently told White that he was going to build the next Spurs team around him.

Later on that year came another shattering incident. December 1964's *Football Monthly* recorded a dramatic image of Dave Mackay suffering a broken leg for the second time in nine months, 20 minutes into a reserve match against Shrewsbury at White Hart Lane.

Incredibly, Mackay was to fight his way back once again, as Bill Nicholson continued to rebuild.

In April 1966 *Football Monthly* showed a Spurs side in transition. From the Double team there was Mackay, Brown, Norman, Henry and Jones. Alongside them were Jimmy Greaves, and the fresh faces of a young Pat Jennings, Phil Beal, Cyril Knowles, Alan Mullery and Greaves' new striking partner, Alan Gilzean, signed from Dundee after he had impressed Bill Nicholson in John White's memorial match.

Just over a year later, with the addition of Terry Venables from Chelsea, Mike England from Blackburn, and youth players Frank Saul and Joe Kinnear, Bill Nicholson turned out what was very nearly another great team.

'Tottenham 1967 – need we say more?' runs the caption over a double page spread of Spurs celebrating their third Cup Final victory of the decade, this one against Chelsea in the first all London final. The match was a personal triumph for Dave Mackay, raising the trophy as captain.

Yet within a year he was off, to Brian Clough's Derby County.

As it happened, the 1966-67 season might have been even more glorious, had Spurs not suffered an error-strewn spell in the autumn, including a rare penalty miss by Jimmy Greaves against West Ham, in one of three consecutive home defeats. Thereafter they rallied well, to finish third in the League with 56 points, more than any other Spurs side since 1961. But without that losing streak, another Double might just have been within grasp.

Almost needless to report, with 25 goals in 38 League games, Greaves was once again leading scorer. 'How long can he stay on the goal standard?' *Football Monthly* asked of its October 1967 cover boy. For another season at least, came Greaves' answer, as he clocked up another 23 League goals in 1967-68. But not one of them was as memorable as Pat Jennings' wind-assisted goalkick that ended up in Manchester United's net in the Charity Shield.

As the 1970s approached, Greaves' picture count in *Football Monthly* remained high. What no one realised was the private battle he was starting to fight with alcohol dependency. Just eight goals in his final season at White Hart Lane followed before he departed as a

makeweight in the £200,000 deal that brought Martin Peters from West Ham in March 1970.

By then there were no members of the Double side left, either. Cover boy for August 1970 was Martin Peters and the team line-up featured in November 1970's magazine contained Martin Chivers, signed for £125,000 from Southampton. Another new face was Ealing born Steve Perryman, featured in March 1971. 'Midfield dynamo Perryman, Spurs most exciting discovery for years, is talked of as a future England international...' wrote Keith Fisher. Even better, surrounded by big money signings, Perryman had come up through the youth team.

But something was happening in football at this time; a shift in tone from panache to pragmatism.

By most standards, managing a club to two League Cups and a UEFA Cup, as Bill Nicholson did in the early 1970s, would count as success. There were individual triumphs too. The *1973-74 Gift Book* devoted a double page picture spread to Pat Jennings, named Footballer of the Year by the Football Writers' Association (an organisation Charlie Buchan had helped to found in 1947).

But for a club with such exacting standards as Spurs, having the best goalkeeper in England was not enough. Increasingly distressed by the growing menace of football hooliganism, the failure of his new side to match their fabulous predecessors and the fear that he was out of touch with the modern footballer, in August 1974 Bill Nicholson resigned.

By pure coincidence, that same month *Football Monthly* also threw in the towel, clearly considered by many former readers to have become similarly out of touch.

The magazine's glory glory days, like those of Tottenham Hotspur were now, alas, in the past.

DANNY BLANCHFLOWER
Spurs and N. Ireland

The champions parade. For the first time in their history Tottenham Hotspur ended a season on top of the First Division. These are the men who brought honour to White Hart Lane—Back row: C. Poynton (trainer), Ramsey, Duquemin, Murphy, Ditchburn, Clarke, Bennett, Withers; Front row: Nicholson, Walters, Willis, Burgess, Baily, Medley.

TOTTENHAM HOTSPUR, 1950-51

OTTENHAM Hotspur's feat of winning the First Division championship and the Second Division title in successive seasons, stamps them as the "team of the year". They join illustrious predecessors in Liverpool (1905-06) and Everton (1931-32).

The secret of the Spurs' success has undoubtedly been team-work. Manager Arthur Rowe describes their play as "push and run football, doing the simple things in the easiest possible way". That calls for team-work of the highest degree.

Their tactics are based on two simple rules. First, when one of the team has the ball, an attack has started. Second, if an opponent is in possession of the ball, the side is on the defensive.

Even when goalkeeper Ted Ditchburn holds the ball in his arms, Spurs are attacking. Players run into position for the ball to be thrown to them. If Alf Ramsey, Ron Burgess or Eddie Baily has the ball at his feet, the same applies. His colleagues take up positions that make it easy for the ball to be passed to them.

In defence, the plan is either to tackle the opponent before he gets the ball under control, or to delay him long enough for the other defenders to take up such positions that there are always two covering the road to goal.

With centre-half Harry Clarke effectively closing the middle like a second edition of Leslie Compton at his best, Spurs' defence is near "goal-proof".

Ramsey, captain and general of the side, and Arthur Willis, his full-back colleague, work and cover one another with almost perfect understanding. With Ditchburn in goal, they made the best rearguard in the League.

In any successful side, there must be an effective link between attack and defence. Spurs have the right man for the job in Eddie Baily, the international inside-left. His midfield wanderings—always with a purpose—and his occasional quick bursts through the defences, have welded the side into a match-winning combination.

Really, Spurs have a seven man-power attack for the wing half-backs, Ron Burgess and Bill Nicholson not only take command in midfield but join in the final assault. The wing-forwards, Sonny Walters and Les Medley too, do not confine their attentions to the touchlines. They close in on goal at the moments when the ball is hovering around the penalty area.

Spear-head of the attack is Len Duquemin, a centreforward from the Channel Islands, and a much better leader than most people imagine. His deft flicks and a habit of taking the opposing centre-half out of position, have led to many Spurs goals.

Spurs are undoubtedly the pattern on which other League clubs have moulded their styles. Their fast movements have also brought back some of the old spectacular appeal to the game, and they have set a fashion that must lead to a big improvement in the general standard of League football.

▲ September 1951 | February 1952 ▶

LEN DUQUEMIN

Tottenham Hotspur

THE FIVE ELMS "GENERAL"

A Profile of the Subject of our Cover Picture

ALF RAMSEY

By
JOHN
THOMPSON

THE team was called Five Elms because that was the name of the street in which most of the boys lived. It was just one of the countless tiny clubs no one ever hears about, the clubs which are more important than anything in football because they are the heart of the game and it would die without them.

Among the eager youths of Five Elms was the dark-haired Dagenham grocer's assistant named Alf Ramsey, who was to become one of the greatest full-backs ever to wear the shirt of Tottenham Hotspur and England . . .

"In those days I never dreamt of ending up in League soccer, let alone being capped," Ramsey has said. But I am told that even then there were hints of the quality which has made him the perfect craftsman—his infinite capacity for self-instruction.

Watch Ramsey in any match and you will see a footballer who, having reached the top of his trade, still regards himself as a pupil of it.

It is Ramsey's diligence, his profiting from trial and error, which have made his style immaculate in appearance and profitable in effect.

During the war, as a sergeant in the Duke of Cornwall's Light Infantry, he was playing so well that he was recommended to Southampton by his commanding officer. Ramsey was then a centre-half, the position occupied at The Dell by Bill Dodgin.

Mr. Dodgin recalls: "It seems odd now to think that I used to move to full back to make way for Alf at centre-half!"

Later Mr. Dodgin, now Fulham's manager, became manager of Southampton. For a time, Ramsey was a subject for experiment. He was even tried as a centre-forward. He proved that he could score goals!

It was early in 1947 that his play began to earn more than local notice. As so often happens in football, the opportunity was caused by another player's misfortune.

Bill Ellerington had been taken ill after an F.A. Cup-tie at Newcastle, and it was during Ellerington's long absence from the team that Ramsey fully revealed his tremendous promise.

About that time, I remember Mr. Dodgin remarking that Ramsey, apart from his skill on the field, was also one of the most intelligent soccer "talkers" he had ever come across.

"Any man who talks football and thinks football every moment of his day, as he does, can't fail to make good," he added.

That was, of course, an early example of the single-mindedness which has been Ramsey's recipe for success.

His transfer to Tottenham Hotspur—in exchange, Southampton received Ernie Jones and a cheque—was finally negotiated by cable because, at the time of the transfer, the Southampton manager was on holiday in Brazil.

At White Hart Lane, Ramsey soon settled comfortably into the Tottenham

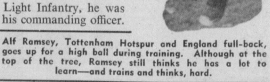

Alf Ramsey, Tottenham Hotspur and England full-back, goes up for a high ball during training. Although at the top of the tree, Ramsey still thinks he has a lot to learn—and trains and thinks, hard.

set-up, still intently studying the game, still insistent that football must be played with careful precision.

His personal view is obvious to all who watch him. To Ramsey the field of play is what a map is to a general. And the map shows the whole picture—not the flanks alone.

For Ramsey the picture is equally broad. He sees the game not only as it affects his own local duties, but as a complete design in which defence and attack and right and left are fluid and must flow together.

The impression that he always has time to spare testifies to his coolness and his imaginative positional play.

His passing is calculated and firm and his refusal to waste the ball, however perplexing the pressure on him, was one clear example for the team-mates with whom he took part in Tottenham's championship triumph.

He owes much to the guidance he has received from manager Arthur Rowe and is grateful for it.

Ramsey, above all, is a conscientious and modest footballer, filled with the conviction—shared by all successful men—that there is always more to learn. . . .

Five Elms and all the other little unknown clubs in which stars are born can be very proud of such a graduate.

" He's from our nursery . . . ! "

CHARLES BUCHAN'S FOOTBALL MONTHLY

1'6

JANUARY 1952

The Magazine of Britain's National Game

Edited by

CHARLES BUCHAN

and

JOHN THOMPSON

ALF RAMSEY
Tottenham Hotspur
& England

PICTURE OF THE SEASON

A goal by Sonny Walters for Tottenham Hotspur against Wolverhampton Wanderers

You need luck and boots that fit!

By ARTHUR ROWE *Manager of Tottenham Hotspur*

THERE are many things I have learned from football and one of them is that you can never finish learning ! And while that is true of most walks of life, football has a rare, and pungent way of reminding us to heed our lessons as we go.

How often, for instance, are we reminded that the refereeing " mistakes " we all think we see have a curious habit of levelling themselves out at the end of a season? What matters, of course, is that the referee is the "' gaffer " on the field and that his decisions are the ones that count.

To get all hot and bothered in disagreement with decisions we cannot alter anyway is really a waste of time—however annoying the incidents may seem. The whistle is the law.

How important it is, too, to play to the whistle—and how often do we see examples of the trouble which comes when players forget this rule.

I remember so very well, being taught this particular lesson so definitely that I never forgot it. It was in a First Division game in the North-East, when I was a Tottenham player.

I recall an opposing winger being badly fouled (as I thought) by one of our defenders. The linesman's flag waved but the winger made a stumbling recovery and while all of us stood still, over came his centre.

The short, little centre-forward rose to it in great style and just as he was making contact I reached up and caught the ball.

Until then, the referee hadn't blown, but he soon did ! He pointed to the penalty spot . . and I'll never forget the look our goalkeeper gave me.

Still with the whistle, but on a happier note . . . how often are we reminded that a game is never lost, or won, till the same whistle has blown for time ! All football followers will have their special memories of thrilling last-minute goals which have decided big matches.

Perhaps some of you will recall the game of this type which stands out most vividly in my own memory. It was a replayed Cup-tie, at Tottenham, against Everton—after a 1-1 draw, at Goodison Park.

With seven minutes to go we were losing 3-1. Our defence had taken a real hammering in the first half, with Everton making us run round in circles. Yet at 3-1, without any apparent hope of victory, we kept cracking.

While thousands of supporters were leaving the ground in disappointment, it happened. Three goals in seven minutes. We had won a game that seemed lost beyond hope.

Sheer courage and refusal to accept defeat till that " last whistle " won that game — and what a terrific joy we all felt at our triumph !

" Tell you what—he can have my house, and I'll come and live with you . . . ."

This fighting spirit is a great asset to any team. There has never been a truly great one without it. A side may be good by virtue of its football ability, but the quality which can lift it to the heights is its team-spirit, its team character.

Players who have the capacity to fight and play their football the way they want to play, as a team, are a wonderful asset. They are the backbone of the game.

I've often heard it said that good players and good teams don't need luck, that they make their own luck. And while it's true that a strong-minded player, or a determined team, will play a way out of a bad patch, there is no doubt that a lucky run of the ball is a telling factor, both for clubs and individuals.

So many times has one seen great players — and great prospects — beaten out of football through the bad luck of a severe injury.

For the best part of two seasons my own club was able to field an almost automatic team each week —because of good fortune with injuries.

What a difference we have experienced this season, during which we have lost three centre-halves in as many weeks, all with similar knee injuries in varying degrees of seriousness.

And here's another illustration of luck . . . in the Spurs' team that won the Second Division championship in 1949-50, Charlie Withers, at left-back, was a " regular."

Having received F.A. recognition, it seemed quite probable that a cap would soon come his way. Then, at the start of the following season, came an injury.

◀◀ April 1952 | February 1952 ▲

" It's a Football Combination game ! "

◀ August 1952 | December 1952 ▲

an operation for removal of a cartilage and two months of playing inactivity.

Arthur Willis, our reserve back, came in. He had cracked away in the reserves without, it seemed, much hope of a senior game. But his chance came and he took it so well that he earned his first international cap against France last October.

Then the wheel turned again. Arthur Willis was injured and had to have his operation for hernia. So Charlie Withers came back to the band. Thus it goes on—in every club, in every season. Truly a hazard of the game !

Remember, too, the part that fortune plays when a lad, sought perhaps by many clubs, makes a choice of the one to which he is to belong perhaps for all his career.

Who knows how his future will work out? Suppose he fulfills his early promise and matures as a professional player. Then comes the anxious waiting for his big chance.

It may come quickly. It may come, too, when his club eleven are a great side. Supported by the fine players who are his team-mates, he will have every chance of success. The team in fact will make him a player.

But what if he makes his debut during one of those lean spells which come to all clubs? Then what of his chances?

Instead of the support of good players, confident players, and a successful team-play he will have to fight for his recognition the hard way. And the hard way in football can be demoralising.

A bad game right at the start may mean the loss of his place. That might be sufficient to knock him back for a season, at least, back to the " forgottens " before he has really been launched.

These, then, are some of the lessons the game has taught me: That luck definitely plays its part in football success and failure; that character and courage will help players and teams to beat off ill-luck when it comes their way; and that, although it is sometimes hard to accept, the good and bad breaks have a habit of levelling themselves out over a period.

I have been taught, too, that a team will make a player more often than a player will make a team. But perhaps the earliest football advice I ever received is probably the soundest I can pass on. It was given to me by my father. He told me, as a boy:

" See your boots are comfortable " and **" use your head."**

I can't better that !

Injury robbed Charlie Withers (left) of a chance of a cap, but it did the reverse for Arthur Willis (right). He replaced the injured Withers in the Tottenham team and was capped against France.

CHARLES BUCHAN'S FOOTBALL

MONTHLY

1/6

JULY 1952

The World's
Greatest Soccer
Magazine

**CONTINENTAL
TOUR EDITION
SPECIAL REPORTS
AND VIVID
PICTURES**

Edited by
Charles Buchan
and
John Thompson

EDDIE BAILY

*Tottenham
and England*

THE PRIDE OF LONDON —EDDIE BAILY

IN the valley, lights sparkled in the streets of the little gold-mining town. Beyond them the dark hills stretched towards the jungle.

A mule train, with bells tinkling, passed along the dusty road. And as I watched it from the veranda I could hear singing from the mining company's palatial club-house.

The chorus was led by a small Cockney footballer named Eddie Baily. And into the mystery of the Brazilian night rose the piercing refrain :

"*All me life I've wanted to be a barrer boy,*

"*A barrer boy I've always wanted to be . . .*"

The contrast was appalling ; the effect a happy one.

In the nearby city of Bello Horizonte that afternoon the English football team had been defeated by an unfancied collection of American amateurs. It was the most embarrassing blow of the whole disastrous World Cup tour.

The team had returned to its quarters in Morro Velho to lick its wounds—and to wonder sadly what folk at home would say when the result was heard.

The descent of a certain amount of gloom could be forgiven. It was inevitable. But the game was over and nothing could be done about it. Mourning would not help.

That, at least, was the attitude of our small Cockney. Unconscious of the fact himself, Eddie Baily, with his homely song and humour, was performing an invaluable service for the morale of the English team.

He was filling the role of "cheerer-upper" which had been taken for so long by Frank Swift.

For the giant from Lancashire and the lightweight Londoner, contrasting as their appearance might be, have this in common : they can grin when others cannot even force a smile.

And that of course is as it should be, for the ability to do just this is the pride of both London and Lancashire.

There is a perky wit in Baily's play as well as in his manner. His football is never obvious. Yet in its subtlety it is never so obscure as to confuse his colleagues.

It personifies the Tottenham gospel of "the simple thing done quickly."

Baily is the most "natural" of footballers. He plays instinctively. I saw the proof of this once when I went to White Hart Lane to help with some cine-camera instructional shots.

Trying to demonstrate a skill of the game Baily at first fumbled. That was because he was thinking out what he did.

In the heat of a game he would have done it without thought, and brilliantly. His natural instinct for football would have permitted it.

It is Baily's naturalness which Mr. Arthur Rowe, distinguished Tottenham manager, emphasises when he talks about his inside-left.

Mr. Rowe says : "Baily's advantage is the natural way he plays the game as we try to teach it at Tottenham. He has a flair for playing *organised* football.

"Believing that the key to football success is not only the quick movement of the ball but the even quicker movement of the player without the ball, Baily is fortunate in having a natural ability for both."

There is, too, a wonderful exuberance about his play which lights up the dullest day. His coolness often amounts to impudence and to London crowds he is probably the most popular of all London footballers.

They like his self-confidence, the alert sparrow-like way in which he holds himself, his dramatic head-clasping when he misses a chance, his boyish glee when he scores.

They like the speed with which he brings a ball under control—a trap and a pass all in one smooth, swift movement.

They like him because he is enjoying the game as much as they are.

And perhaps most of all, they like him because he is the kid next door

"I'm the vice captain."

who became famous—and never noticed the difference.

Once Baily almost became a Chelsea player. But his heart has always been anchored securely at White Hart Lane. As a boy from Clapton he would stand and hero-worship Willie Hall, the man upon whom he has tried to model his own play.

He told me once : "While still at school I'd never miss a match at White Hart Lane in which Willie was playing. I'd hardly take my eyes off him, studying every move he made so that I could go back and try to copy him in kids' games."

The day after Baily made that remark a fair-haired young man on crutches went into the Tottenham dressing-room. Crippled Willie Hall, one of the greatest inside-forwards the game has known, had come to wish good luck to the unknown boy who was nervously awaiting his first game for the mighty London club.

Baily has travelled far since then, adding laurels to his reputation as recently as the English victory over Austria in Vienna. But I doubt if he will forget the old international's gesture—or his example.

As a soldier he played for the British Army of the Rhine, signing professional forms for Tottenham in October, 1947, and gaining his first cap against Spain in Rio de Janeiro.

He will doubtless always be a Tottenham player. It is difficult to imagine him in any colours except the white shirt with the fighting cock emblem which symbolises his own spirit so well.

It is the spirit of a young Cockney who sang to cheer the gloom away from a beaten team one night in Brazil.

▲ July 1952

BILL NICHOLSON
Tottenham Hotspur and England

AN OPEN LETTER From

The Right Hon. LORD MORRISON, P.C., D.L., President of Tottenham Hotspur F.C.

Dear Charles Buchan,

You have asked me to write something about football for your excellent magazine. Well, here we go!

First I must warn you that I am going way back a long time, to the good old days when, as a Scottish schoolboy, I played two matches every Saturday. I was a halfback in the morning and a forward in the afternoon.

In those far-off days little did I dream of the exciting things that were to come my way in later life—twenty years as Member of Parliament for Tottenham and, after that, signed by the House of Lords on a free transfer!

I would not claim that football is a main topic of conversation in the House of Lords, but you will be surprised to learn that football topics are often discussed at the lunch table.

I have even known Lord Bishops to join in the argument and disclose a useful knowledge of the game.

It used to be something of a mystery to many Peers why the Marquess of Londonderry, whose political views are not exactly the same as mine, should often choose a quiet corner of the Lords library to hold earnest consultation with me.

The answer was easy, although many of their Lordships would never have guessed it—we are both life-long lovers of football. We discuss football problems even in the solemnity of the House of Lords.

During the recent General Election, I am sorry to relate, my enthusiasm caused annoyance to one of my colleagues. I was sitting pondering over the chances of Spurs beating Sunderland away, when he came over to me and asked: "Well, who's going to win?" I unhesitatingly said "Spurs."

He said: "My dear fellow, I'm not talking about your silly game. I'm asking about the General Election."

Where I went to school, football was strictly prohibited. I can still recall the schoolmaster loudly telling us: "Look here, you boys, I'm here to teach you to read and write, not to kick the toes out of your boots playing football."

In spite of his prohibition, perhaps because of it, I played two matches every Saturday, and evening games when light permitted.

This brings me to describe my first big football adventure. I hope it may help the younger generation to realise what a mighty change has come over school life with regard to sport.

Sauntering slowly home from school, a placard in a grocer's shop window caught my eye:

HOSPITAL SATURDAY SPORTS
FIVE-A-SIDE FOOTBALL COMPETITION
OPEN TO SCHOOLBOYS
SILVER MEDALS TO THE WINNERS

In less than two hours, I had rounded up four other boys, called at the secretary's house and entered our team for the competition.

Preliminary ties had to be played in the evenings,

Lord Morrison

reserving the final as the big event of the Sports.

On Monday evening we played our first round and won easily, 4-1. The Secretary instructed us to return for the second round, on Wednesday.

Unfortunately for us, after we had left for home the date of our next tie was changed from Wednesday to Thursday and as the Secretary did not know our address he wrote to the schoolmaster asking him to "tell your school team of the alteration."

Next morning, the balloon went up! As soon as prayers were over he produced the letter and demanded to know the boys who played in a football competition last evening.

"Whose idea was this?" he thundered, looking sternly in my direction, and meekly I replied: "Mine, sir."

"Does your father know about this? What did he say about it?" In a trembling voice I said: "Please, sir, when he heard we won the first round he was very happy."

My reply almost drove him to distraction. "Happy!", he gasped. "Very happy! Your father must be a bigger idiot than you. Tell him from me that education means developing your brains, not your feet."

With that final shot, he tore up the letter and said: "Come to my room. I'll give you enough home-work to keep you from football for a long time."

That evening we five went into a long huddle and finally decided to see it through. While the others did their extra home-work I went to the Secretary's house and found out what was in the letter.

We played the second round and won 3-0, which put us in the Final for Saturday afternoon. Before a big crowd, we romped home by 3-1 and modesty forbids me to tell you who scored two of the goals. Proudly we lined up to receive our silver medals.

Many a time since then, when presenting football cups and medals to schoolboys, I have thought of the transformation since those days .... five boys afraid to go to school on Monday morning, wondering anxiously whether the schoolmaster had heard, scared to bring our medals in case he threw them in the fire. . . . !

Nowadays, the whole school would get a half-holiday in honour of the occasion!

You will be pleased to know that my first great football adventure ended more happily than we anticipated. After prayers, the schoolmaster ordered us to his room, slowly produced from his pocket the local morning newspaper and read the headline to us:

HOSPITAL SPORTS — WINNING SCHOOLBOYS PLAY
CLEVER FOOTBALL

Looking sadly across the table at us, he said: "So you defied me. You played. You won—I lost. Well, I'm not angry with you any more. Let's shake hands and be friends."

Wishing you good health and your magazine good luck,

Yours sincerely, MORRISON

I wasn't a great success but.....

it did give the funny men of the team a chance for a laugh at my expense

says Ron Burgess when telling of the time he was chosen for outside left. He continues, " When I walked into the dressing-room to change, half-a-dozen left boots were lined up near my peg. In each boot was stuck a card bearing words such as: 'This boot for taking corner kicks.' 'This boot for a dry ground.' 'This one for a wet ground.' 'This boot for putting the ball over the bar,' etc. etc. They had also laid out a strip of cocoanut matting so that I could have some sprinting practice before taking the field."

This is only one of the many amusing stories with which Ron Burgess enlivens the 212 pages of his book, FOOTBALL—MY LIFE.

Acclaimed as one of the best soccer biographies for years. It has everything to entertain you.

DRAMA   Internationals at Hampden, Ninian, Wembley—Continental tours—Championship and Cup battles—wartime football—the star studded R.A.F. side—Great Britain v. Rest of Europe—behind the scenes of professional football—Ron tells you honestly of them all, successes and failures.

PHOTOGRAPHS

These are but three of 32 pages of pictures, including a historic memento of the Great Britain v. Rest of Europe match, autographed by the entire team.

HUMOUR

The amusing incidents on and off the field. The Welsh team's mysterious horseshoe—arrest by police—leg-pulling among the R.A.F. stars—internationals in the luggage rack—6d. fee for article.

CONTROVERSY

Views on much publicised dirty play—rough Continental tactics—referees—reform of the laws—substitutes—my best teams.

WHAT THE PRESS SAYS

Charles Buchan's " Football Monthly "   Ron Burgess is a favourite with crowds everywhere because of his sportsmanship, his enormous enthusiasm and splendid spirit and because those qualities are finely expressed in his book his story can be heartily recommended to all who follow the game.
Sunday Pictorial   A stirring story well worth any football fan's 7/6.
World Sports   Honest . . . many sidelights for the connoisseur . . . will be appreciated.
Sporting Record   The story of the ideal footballer.
Welsh Western Mail   Most interesting book that should prove decidedly popular with fans.
Also recommended by Desmond Hackett—Daily Express ; Willie Evans—Daily Mirror ; Roy Peskett—Daily Mail ; Eric Wright—Reynolds News ; and many others.

At only 7/6 this is a Christmas 'must' for every Soccer fan

Get it now!

Football - my life

by RON BURGESS

published by Souvenir Press Ltd., 81 Peters Court, London, W.2.
From any bookseller or from the publishers.

For your album...

LESLIE BENNETT
Tottenham Hotspur

SPOTLIGHT ON

TOTTENHAM HOTSPUR

EVERYONE, of course, knows Tottenham Hotspur as the Spurs. But not many know why they got the nickname.

It dates back from the days when the club was founded, in 1882, on Tottenham Marshes.

One of the members had been reading about the exploits of the Earl of Northumberland's son, Henry Percy, nicknamed Hotspur.

So he proposed, at a meeting held under a lamp-post in Northumberland Avenue, that the club should be named Hotspur. That quickly became abbreviated to Spurs.

Now they are one of the most famous and richest clubs in the land—and a household word in the game.

Look at their successes in the last few years. Champions of the Second Division in 1950, champions of the First Division in 1951 and runners-up last May.

That was brought about by a brand of football that has not only been successful,

but has also provided bright entertainment on every ground they have visited.

It has been called "push and run" football. It is, with every player pushing the ball first time and running into position to receive a pass from a colleague.

But it needs great players to carry out the policy.

Spurs have these great players. Ted Ditchburn is one of the best goalkeepers never to have received a full England international cap; Alf Ramsey, without peer as a full-back; Bill Nicholson and Welsh international Ron Burgess, the wing half-backs and backbone of the side; Alf Clarke, tall, defensive centre-half, who will one day be England's first choice; and Sonny Walters, Les Bennett, Len Duquemin, Eddie Baily and Les Medley—on their days the best attacking forward line in the country.

Yes, Spurs have a team worth a king's ransom in transfer fees. They are serving

up a brand of football that is bringing many imitators.

Because it is the kind the public wants to see.

It is somewhat reminiscent of the old Corinthian days when the ball went from man to man with remarkable speed.

There is one slight flaw in an otherwise great side. Often Spurs do not get the full rewards of their combined skill because they miss chances in front of goal.

But that can be forgiven while they continue to delight the thousands who go to see them by their clever approach work.

A few minutes of the Spurs' artistry is worth an hour of the "kick and rush" stuff that one so often sees nowadays.

It may be that Tottenham have not carried all before them this season. That is because they had a strenuous tour in Canada and the United States last summer, and they are feeling the after effects.

But, under the management of the astute Arthur Rowe, a Spurs' centre-half

Tottenham Hotspur : Standing—Nicholson, Ramsey, Duquemin, Ditchburn, Clarke, Bennett, Wetton. Sitting—McClellan, Walters, Willis, Baily, Withers, Medley. Insets (left), Rowe (right), Burgess.

▲ April 1953

in the middle '30's, when they earned the name of " Greyhounds " by their fast, penetrative methods, Spurs will soon be among the honours again.

They have a wealth of talent, like Charlie Withers, Melvyn Hopkins, Toni Marchi, Colin Brittan, Ralph Wetton, Sid McClellan and Tommy Harmer (a wizard with the ball) ready to step into the places of the present stars.

They will have no need to trade in the expensive transfer market to keep them in the top rank. Spurs have built wisely and on a solid foundation.

Right from the start, Spurs made a name for themselves. For the first ten years of their life they were one of the best amateur sides in the South of England, until, in 1893, they committed a " crime."

They gave one of their players—Payne by name—10s. to buy a pair of football boots. For this, the London Football Association suspended the club for a fortnight and the player for a week.

So Spurs turned professional and applied for membership of the Southern League. But they were not then the popular club they are to-day. Their application received only one vote.

They were admitted to the Southern League, in 1898, and soon had the Soccer world talking. For, three years later, they won the F.A. Cup, beating Sheffield United in the final after a replay.

They were the first professional club to break the Northern monopoly and bring the Cup south.

There are many stories told of the wonderful Spurs team that won the Cup in 1901. Of the great defence, Clawley, Erentz and Tait ; of half-backs Morris, Hughes and Jones ; and forwards like Smith, Cameron, Brown, Copeland and Kirwan.

Comparisons are made with the Spurs of to-day. But it is enough to give the old Spurs due credit for their marvellous performance. They were on their own in their day.

Spurs continued as one of the leading lights of the Southern League until 1908. Then they had ambitions of joining the Football League which was *the* competition.

So they resigned from the Southern League and applied for admission to the Football League. Their application was turned down.

The rejected Spurs looked to be in trouble. Fortunately for them, Stoke City resigned and Spurs got their place.

Once among the elect, Spurs made their presence felt. They won promotion to the First Division in their first season. They stayed in the top circle until 1915, when they were relegated.

When football restarted after the first World War, it was thought that Spurs would be given a place in the extended First Division, but Arsenal and Chelsea were given preference.

Spurs made light of the League's disapproval. They ran away with the Second Division championship in the first postwar season, with a record total of 70 points from the 42 games played.

What's more, they followed it up by winning the F.A. Cup the following season. All Spurs supporters will recall the Jimmy Dimmock goal by which they beat Wolves in the final, at Stamford Bridge.

This was another era of Spurs' greatness. Under the inspiring leadership of Arthur Grimsdell, one of the greatest-ever left half-backs, and with players, such as Tommy Clay, Bert Smith, Jimmy Seed, Jimmy Cantrell, Bert Bliss and Dimmock, they swept all before them.

But at that time, Spurs did not keep pace with the times. As the players aged together, their powers slumped until in

"I thought young Reg Fruin shaped well—real venom in some of them 'Can't you see that, ref ? '"

1928 they were again relegated to the Second Division.

On this occasion, they were unlucky. They had gained 38 points when they finished their matches rather early in the season. As 34 points was considered a safe margin, Spurs left for a Continental trip before the closing day of the season.

While they were abroad, they learned that Sunderland had won at Middlesbrough and pushed them down.

It was a shock from which they recovered quickly. In five years, with players like Bill Felton, Bill Whatley, Arthur Rowe, Taffy O'Callaghan, George Hunt and Willie Evans, they won promotion again.

It was the season which saw the rise to fame of Willie Hall, the great fair-haired inside-left, who played for England, and had the great misfortune to lose both his legs through thrombosis.

Within two years they were back again in the Second Division, where, despite changes of management, players and tactics, they remained for fifteen years, until 1950.

During some of these years, Spurs had as manager Peter McWilliam, Scottish international half-back. He moulded the present successful Spurs' style.

Now they have Arthur Rowe, who guided the team to the top of the tree. They have never looked back since.

Many grand players who built undying reputations have assisted Spurs.

Pride of them all was Vivian J. Woodward, holder of more than sixty England caps in both amateur and professional internationals.

Then there were the brothers Steel, Herbert Chapman, afterwards one of the greatest managers the game has known, Frank Osborne, general manager of Fulham, Walter Bull, Tiny Joyce, the mighty 16st. goalkeeper, Ralph Ward, a hard-hitting right-back, Fanny Walden, smallest and most elusive of wing forwards, Bert Middlemiss and Jimmy Elkes.

The names reel off the tongue, bringing memories of the countless great games at White Hart Lane like the never-to-be-forgotten F.A. Cup-tie with Everton.

Spurs are an institution.

CHARLES
BUCHAN'S
FOOTBALL
MONTHLY

1/6

JUNE, 1953

TED DITCHBURN

*Tottenham Hotspur
and England*

BACKS MUST BE SAFE AND TWO-FOOTED

By ALF RAMSEY
Spurs and England

MISTAKES made by full-backs can turn victory into defeat. Except for the goalkeeper, they are the last line of defence and should mould their style accordingly. Safety-first must be the slogan.

The whole secret is correct positional play. A back, for instance, must know exactly what his goalkeeper, his partner, the half-back in front of him, and, in fact, all the side, are doing.

Let me deal with each one separately. First, the goalkeeper. When he advances to meet a cross from the right-wing, it is the right-back's job to cover him by taking up position on the goal-line.

If the goalkeeper shouts for the ball, let him have it. But move into a position where you can deal with any other threat to the goal.

Then you must have an understanding with your partner. When he goes upfield, I, as a right-back, make a point of covering both him and the centre-half. I must not be caught square, or one well-timed through pass will find the goal uncovered.

And I always get into position to receive a ball from him. It may not come, but at least I know I am in position to help.

Now to the man in front of me. With the Spurs, it's Bill Nicholson, of course. Well, he takes the inside-forward so that I can concentrate on the wing-forward.

My main object is to keep in such close contact with Nicholson that I can cut off any pass intended for the wing-forward. It means a close study of your colleague's style.

There are times when the wing-forward gets the ball before I can get near enough to intercept it. Then it is my job to see that the winger does as little damage as possible.

So I keep him out on the touch-line whenever possible. Not only is there no danger to the goal there, but it gives time for my defensive colleagues to take up position.

One thing a full-back must not do in these circumstances is to rush in for a quick tackle. He will be easily beaten if the opponent has the ball under control.

Always, if possible, try to form a second line of defence with the centre-half. Cover him whenever possible.

Above all, if beaten, get back to goal as quickly as possible. Quick recovery is the hall-mark of a full-back.

You must be able to use both feet equally well. In fact, a right-back should be stronger with the left foot.

When clearing, the ball must be placed to a colleague. Low, whenever possible, so that defence can be turned into attack with one well-placed kick.

You cannot be too expert at kicking, heading, trapping the ball and the other finer points.

Practise until you are well-nigh perfect. And practise at close quarters, just as if an opponent were rushing down on you.

Programme Exchange Corner will appear again in " Football Monthly " next month—on sale June 18. Make sure of your copy by placing an order with your newsagent NOW.

ALF RAMSEY.

▲ June 1952

Tottenham Hotspur centre-half, tells how he broke into football—and gives his verdict

IT'S A GRAND LIFE !

AT nine o'clock one Saturday morning in March, 1949, I had the surprise of my life.

I had reported at the Tottenham Hotspur ground to travel to Brighton for a reserve match, when Mr. Jimmy Anderson, who was then acting as manager, summoned me to his office.

"How do you feel about playing in the League side against Luton?" he asked me.

As I was Spurs' reserve centre-half, you may wonder why Jimmy troubled to seek my opinion. Simply, it was this.

I had signed for Spurs a bare fortnight earlier, and had played only two games in the reserve team. Jimmy naturally wanted to know if I thought I was ready.

Of course, I was dumbstruck at the prospect of stepping into Spurs' League team, which was at that time challenging for promotion.

But there was only one answer to Jimmy's question, for in football, as in everything else, opportunity must never be spurned.

Nevertheless, although I took the chance Jimmy offered me, I couldn't help feeling it *had* come a bit too soon.

Apart from the two reserve games for Spurs, my experience had been confined to Southern League and Welsh League football with Lovell's Athletic.

It was a tremendous test for one so raw, but good fortune was with me.

A new player depends as much upon his colleagues as himself in surviving his first exacting test.

It was my good luck to step into a middle line flanked by Billy Nicholson and Ronnie Burgess, as fine a combination of wing-half-backs as League football can boast.

It meant that I was given adequate cover, and was not subjected to excessive pressure. We won 2—1, and I kept my place for the rest of that season.

We failed to gain promotion, but when the next campaign opened we had Alf Ramsey, from Southampton, at right-back.

In my first full season as a League player, I found myself the pivot of a defence in which every other player was a star.

Ramsey formed a first-class full-back partnership with Charlie Withers, in front of Ted Ditchburn, as brilliant a goalkeeper as I have ever seen.

And, as I have said, my supporting wing-halves could not have been bettered.

It seemed too good to be true.

Well, we won the Second Division championship that season and, in the following campaign, carried off the League title.

They were two wonderful seasons for us and I had the good fortune to play in every match.

In fact, from the day of my debut against Luton, I played in ninety-four successive League matches—until I was injured in a public trial game !

The "man-for-man" marking system introduced by Arthur Rowe, our present manager, has been a great help to me at centre-half.

It simplifies my work, and frees me from the doubts that worry many defenders.

My sole task, in the defensive sense, is to mark the opposing centre-forward. If he roves to either wing, I go with him.

▲ December 1953

This roving practice, adopted by many centre-forwards, leaves a gap in midfield through which one of the inside-forwards usually streaks.

That's the moment when a centre-half can be caught in two minds, wondering whether to stick to his centre-forward or leave him and tackle the onrushing inside-forward.

I have the advantage of knowing that my wing-halves will keep check on each of their opposing inside-forwards, and that the centre-forward is the only opponent I need worry about.

That is the general defensive plan, although there are times, of course, when a sudden emergency calls for action outside the blueprint scheme.

I'm satisfied, from my own experience, that close marking is absolutely essential.

A centre-forward should never be allowed to turn with the ball. If he is the type of player who exploits latitude of this kind, the centre-half will be in trouble time and time again.

Here's a personal story to illustrate my meaning.

After the injury I have mentioned, I returned to Spurs' team in a game against Newcastle, in the F.A. Charity Shield.

I was a bit wary over my injured knee and was inclined to stand off a little from Jackie Milburn, Newcastle's centre-forward.

It was the worst thing I could have done. Milburn, perhaps more than any other centre-forward, rejoices in elbow-room and, in a flash, he had turned towards the touchline with the ball.

My efforts to dispossess him were futile and, in quick time, the ball was in our net.

It happened that we scored two goals to beat Newcastle, but Milburn's goal taught me a lesson.

Had I been marking him closely enough, he would never have broken away.

The faster a centre-forward moves, the tighter you have to hold him. I don't agree with the theory that the centre-half is better placed if he occupies a position between his own goal and the centre-forward.

It's a fallacy to believe that you must

"Now aren't you glad I gave you my measles?"

BILLY NICHOLSON

RON BURGESS

have the advantage if you keep on the "goal-side" of him.

The man with the ball has the advantage and, if you give a good centre-forward an inch of rope, he'll be away before you can get to grips with him.

So much for the tactical side of football. Now let me tell you of the events that led me into League Soccer.

When at school at Woodford Bridge, I played for Woodford Boys and supported West Ham United.

I was a centre-half even in those days and, from the railings at Upton Park, I used to watch big Jim Barrett, Ted Fenton and Dick Walker playing at centre-half for West Ham at various times.

Each was a master in the pivotal position and I picked up a lot of valuable points by studying their methods.

It was always my ambition to become a professional footballer, but in those days I never seriously believed that it would be realised.

In fact, the war, in 1939, threatened to end my football altogether.

There was no organised football for boys in our district after the start of hostilities and, it is a fact, that for four years I did not play in a match of any kind.

We managed to have a kickabout among ourselves, but that was little more than recreation.

Then I joined the R.A.F., and my football horizon brightened.

I found myself playing among professionals whose comments encouraged me to think I had a chance of making the grade.

My biggest step forward came when I was stationed in the Chippenham district. A pal persuaded me to write to Lovell's Athletic for a trial.

It worked, and, after a brief spell as an amateur, Lovell's signed me on professional forms.

Lovell's play at Newport but I managed to get away from my station regularly to play for them. We had a grand team in those days—I well remember our Cup run of season 1945-46.

The games were played in two legs that season and, in the first round proper, we knocked out Bournemouth. Next came a double victory over Bath City. Then we found ourselves drawn against mighty Wolves.

They beat us 4—2 at Newport, and

crushed us by 8—1 at Molineux. Never shall I forget that away tie.

Billy Wright, playing inside-left, scored two of the goals, and Jimmy Mullen, his partner, half-volleyed the ball into our net with as powerful a shot as I've ever seen.

For me, personally, the outstanding recollection of that Cup series was the match I missed. It was the first leg of the Bath tie, at Newport.

I used to travel by rail between Chippenham and Newport, changing at Bristol. The week before the Bath Cup-tie I was making the usual change, on my return journey from Newport, when I was asked by the military authorities on the station to produce my Service pass.

I hadn't got one!

They gave me seven days' C.B., and, on the following Saturday, I was on fatigue duties instead of taking my usual place at centre-half for Lovell's in the Cup-tie!

When my war service ended I took a job in the chocolate-making department of Lovell's factory, and continued to play for the works team. I stayed with the club until Spurs came on the scene.

Bill Whatley, their old Welsh international full-back, who still holds an official position with the club, watched me in a couple of games, and Jimmy Anderson also saw me play before they made me a firm offer.

And that seems to get back to where my story started.

I've had a grand time with the Spurs and have never regretted joining them.

Everything is done in first-class style at Tottenham, and careful attention is given to the welfare of the players.

Playing for Spurs has also enabled me to travel abroad in luxury.

In less than five years with the club I've been to Germany, Denmark, Belgium, France, Canada and the United States.

And that gives me my cue for a tail-end story.

We were stripping in our dressing-room in Copenhagen, when we were told that the match, against a local representative team, would have to be postponed.

The reason was that heavy rain was keeping the attendance figure down.

It may be wonderful, wonderful Copenhagen, but there's a lot to be said for places like London, Birmingham and Manchester.

You can be pretty sure a football match will be played, even if it is raining!

A CUP OVERFLOWING WITH THRILLS . . .

One of the countless thrills that have enlivened the F.A. Cup competition of 1952-53 . . . Gilbert Merrick, of Birmingham City, punches clear from Len Duquemin, of Tottenham Hotspur, in the 2-2 replay at White Hart Lane.

▲ May 1953

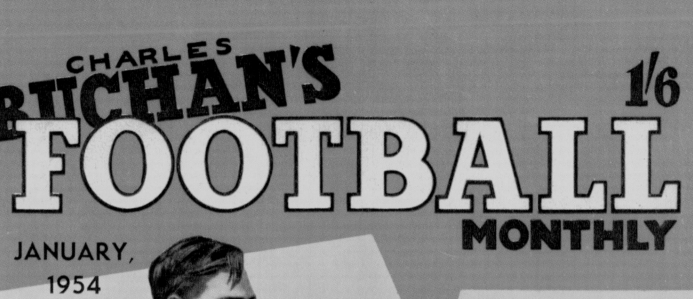

CHARLES BUCHAN'S
FOOTBALL
MONTHLY

1/6

JANUARY,
1954
No. 29

INSIDE: Stanley
Matthews in Colour

Exclusive Articles
and Action Shots

Special New
Year Issue

GEORGE ROBB
Tottenham Hotspur
and England

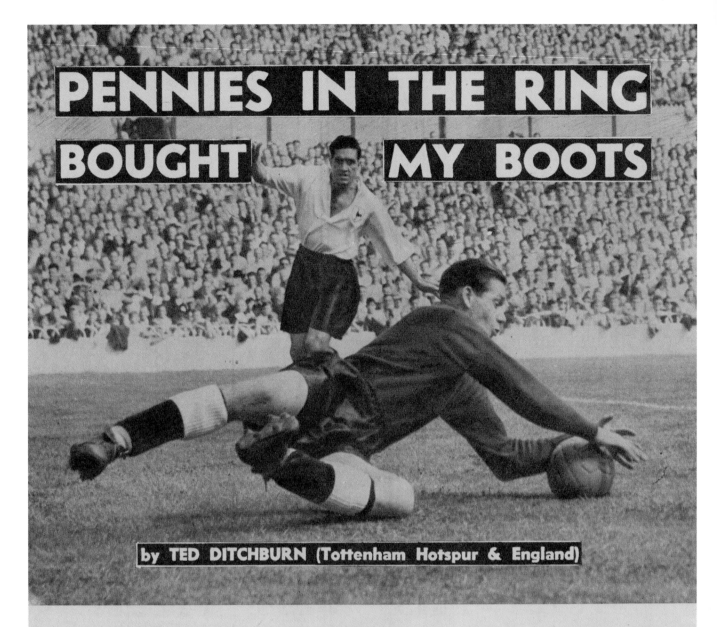

PENNIES IN THE RING BOUGHT MY BOOTS

by TED DITCHBURN (Tottenham Hotspur & England)

IT all began one Friday afternoon at Lawn-road Boys' School, Northfleet. The sports master decided that I was to keep goal for the school second team on the following day.

"And none of your tea-garden tricks," he added, after breaking the news to me. Precisely what he meant by that remark, I still don't know. I can only assume it had some reference to an incident that, even then, I had long forgotten.

Now a place in the school team, even though it was only the second eleven, was something new for me. Until I was twelve, I was not really interested in football . . . but I was boxing mad.

As a schoolboy, I used to fight at Rochester Casino. Another boy and I would appear at the foot of a professional bill as an " added attraction." And when the bout was over, the crowd would throw money into the ring for us.

That's how I was able to buy my first pair of boxing boots.

Whether I should ever have made the grade as a professional boxer, I shouldn't care to say. That can only remain a matter of conjecture.

The simple fact is that the sports master's decision to try me as goalkeeper in the school second team was instrumental in diverting my sporting interests from the ring to the football field.

FROM that day to this, I have been a goalkeeper . . . with one fleeting exception. In one school match we were hard pressed to field a team, and to help the cause, I played at centre-forward.

We were beaten, I scored no goals, and my performance as a forward was nothing to shout about. I was, in fact, restored to the goalkeeping position in the next match, a significant reflection on my display as leader of the attack !

In my first season as goalkeeper in the Lawn-road School team, I was picked for Northfleet Boys. I was also given the captaincy of the town boys' team, and by this time was beginning to think seriously about the goalkeeping business.

Things were going well for me, and I was quite happy to sacrifice my boxing ambitions. I gained a place in the Kent Boys' team, and then came the tremendous thrill of a place in the international schoolboys' trial.

I played for the South against the Midlands at Slough. Alas, we lost 4—2, and selection for the England Boys' team was not for me.

"FROM Programme Boy to Pro" was the title of a boys' football novel I once read. Well, truth is sometimes just as strange as fiction—for that experience was actually mine.

Yes, I was once a programme boy . . . for the old Northfleet club, which served Spurs as a nursery before the war.

I was a keen follower of the club, and by selling programmes and helping to deliver groceries to the caterers at the Stonebridge-road ground, I was allowed in to see the matches without paying.

To an enthusiastic schoolboy, it was a sound business proposition,

▲ October 1954

and I also had the satisfaction of knowing I was helping the club.

I was not alone in this activity. With me was George Piper, who was afterwards on Spurs' books for a time, and later played for Gillingham.

After leaving school I took a job in a paper mill at Northfleet, and played for the mill team in the Gravesend Borough League. Then it was that I was spotted by Ben Ives, the old Spurs scout.

★

I CAME to Tottenham, full of hope and wonderment, on a three-weeks' trial. Much has happened since then, but I recall clearly that vital stage of my football life.

I remember a private work-out on the St. Ignatius playing field, at the rear of Tottenham's ground. Behind my goal stood an onlooker, who gave me several scraps of advice.

It was Andy Thompson, the old Spurs forward, who was on the training staff of Chelsea until last year. Andy's help that day meant a lot— it gave me confidence and lessened the tension that most young trialists feel.

Everything was going to plan. I was taken on Spurs' ground staff, and given a place in Northfleet's amateur side. After three matches I was promoted to the Kent League team—a rate of progress beyond my wildest hope.

It was an unusual situation. Spurs spotted young players from all over the British Isles, and sent them to their Northfleet nursery for development.

I had been picked up on the Northfleet doorstep, taken to Tottenham and then switched for grooming to my own home-town. I felt on top of the world.

★

IT was in 1939 that I signed professional forms for Spurs. A number of us, including Les Bennett and Les Stevens, were brought up from the Northfleet nursery to Tottenham.

We reported for training a few weeks before the opening of the season, but our new experience of life as fully-fledged professional footballers was remarkably brief. The season had been in progress one week when the war broke out and big football was brought to an abrupt stop.

At that time I was third choice goalkeeper at Tottenham, and when regional football started there was little chance for a player of my limited experience. Spurs, like most League clubs, were able to field one team only, and their senior goalkeeper was Percy Hooper.

Rather than waste my time hanging about for a chance that might not come, I went on loan to Dartford, the Southern League club, and gained some useful experience with them.

At 18, I volunteered for the R.A.F. That meant service on a variety of stations, and I managed to play football fairly regularly.

I shall always remember the time when I went on a P.T. course at Cosford. Bert Williams, Wolves' international goalkeeper, was on the staff there, and was, of course, the star performer in the station team.

With Bert about, my chances of a game in goal were nil, and the same went for Reg Savage, the old Leeds United goalkeeper, who was on the course with me.

It was in 1941 that I was given my first game in Tottenham's war-time side. After that I managed an odd game now and then, but it was not until season 1943-44, when I was stationed at East Ham, that I was playing regularly for Spurs.

That season, by the way, was the best I have ever had. I was picked for the England team that beat Scotland 6—2 at Wembley, and also played against Wales at Cardiff.

On top of that I played in three F.A. sides and appeared in the R.A.F. representative team. Yes, I feel sure that was my most notable season, even though football was only on a war-time basis.

Well, I have had a lot to say about myself. Now for a few comments on the job of goalkeeping.

Most important to the man between the posts is the quality of the defenders in front of him. At Tottenham, I have been fortunate enough to enjoy the protection offered by a shield of top-class players. Defenders, particularly the centre-half and full-backs, can make or break a goalkeeper.

The goalkeeper's job is quite different from any other on the field. During much of the play he is isolated from the rest of his team. His job limits his area of activity to the goalmouth, and he is an easy target for spectators who like to air their views.

I try to ignore the crowd, even when the ball is at the other end of the field. The slightest distraction can be fatal to a goalkeeper, and he must exert every nerve in his efforts to concentrate on his job of work on the field.

It isn't always easy, of course. The crowd is so close, particularly on grounds where the net stretches practically to the barrier, that he cannot miss some of the comments.

Vocal response of the right kind has an encouraging effect, of course. A roar of applause inspires a feeling of confidence, and as a goalkeeper, I have often been helped by the crowd.

However much I try to shut the noise of the crowd out of my mind, there is one voice at Tottenham I cannot help hearing. Often, as I am clearing a ball at the Park-lane end, one staunch supporter booms " Good old Bank of England ! " in stentorian tones for my particular benefit.

It's a friendly voice, and the owner is no fair-weather fan. I hear his call in good times and bad.

Ditchburn gets a worm's-eye view of the ball as he stands on his head saving a fierce shot.

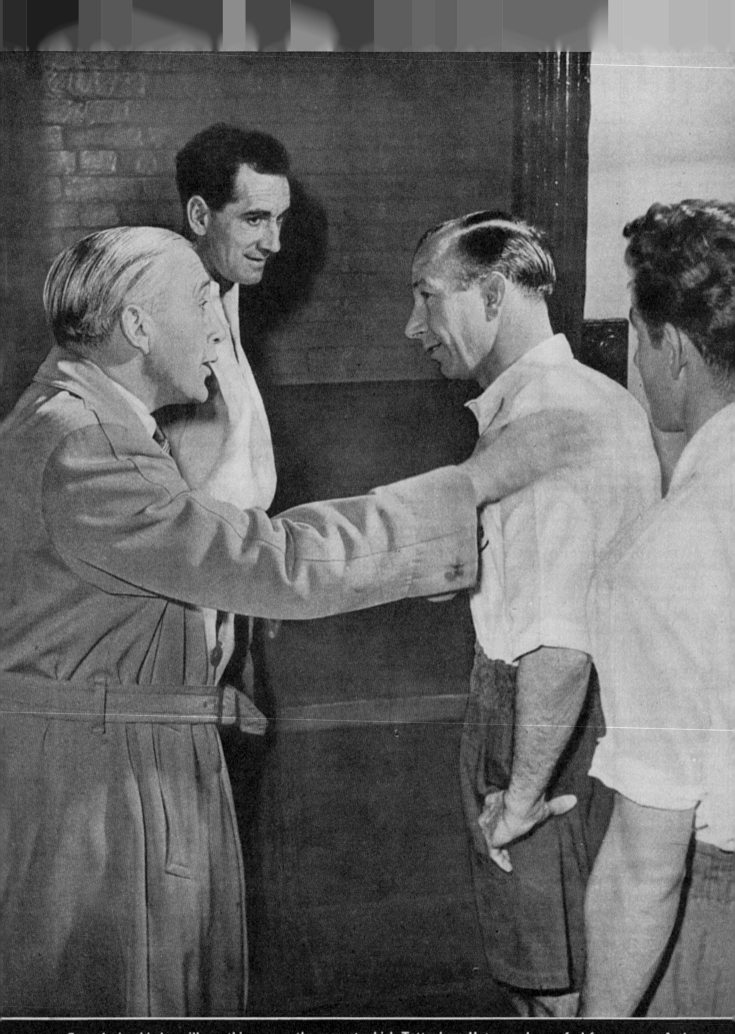

Even during his long illness this season, the respect which Tottenham Hotspur players feel for manager Arthur Rowe has inspired them to put all they know into their games. In this study of a dressing-room scene just before M. Rowe is giving a final word of advice to his captain, Ronnie Burgess.

Robb Robbed!

Foiled by a desperately daring dive by Sunderland's Willie Fraser, Spurs' left-winger George Robb, leaps high in the air to clear the rolling goalkeeper.

◀ April 1954 | May 1954 ▲

WHY I CHANGED ••• MY STYLE •••

By
Ronnie Burgess
Tottenham Hotspur
and Wales

FOOTBALL has provided me with a wealth of thrills. Moments of triumph have come my way, and of course, I have had my disappointments. But, first, I must tell you of the greatest difficulty I have been called upon to face during my career.

Until two or three seasons ago I was recognised as an attacking wing-half-back. This has always been my natural game, but Father Time has a habit of taking his toll of one's physical strength.

I have had quite a long run in the game, and it was obvious a couple of years ago that I would have to conserve my strength.

That's why my attacking bent had to be curbed, and my all-out dashes into the opposition goalmouth made less frequently.

Even then, after settling to a more conservative type of wing-half game, I had the utmost difficulty in resisting the urge to go through. But the change in style was a sound move, and I'm sure it is a way any player can lengthen his career.

Naturally, I am a strong advocate of attacking wing-half play. The value to his side of the raiding wing-half is tremendous. But his raids should not be made without discrimination.

He should seek to surprise the opposition with a sudden dash, and should time it for a moment when the defence is spread-eagled.

Having spotted the gap, he should flash through, provided an understanding exists for a colleague to be on hand to cover his own position.

I have managed to score some valuable goals by this means, although, of course, my scoring plan has more often miscarried.

Even when the sudden, forward burst of a wing-half fails in its object, it brightens the game, and I know from the crowd reaction I have myself experienced that spectators find it an enjoyable diversion from the orthodox plan of play.

▲ 1954–55 Gift Book

After a thirteen-minute hold-up the referee decided to make a start. Picture shows the waterlogged Tottenham pitch before the replay with Leeds United.

The value of the attacking wing-half was demonstrated to me in my first game in League football.

I was given my first big chance at right-half for Spurs in a Second Division match at Norwich in February, 1939.

We were a goal down at half-time, scored by Jack Acquroff, the Norwich centre-forward, who, oddly enough, had started his career with Spurs some years earlier.

George Ludford, our centre-forward, equalised, and then came the tense struggle for the winner. It looked a draw until Vic Buckingham, our left-half, who is now manager of West Bromwich Albion, saw his chance.

He gathered the ball smartly, and instead of making the expected pass, took it goalwards before crashing it into the net with a strong cross-drive.

Vic had given me an object-lesson, although it was not his practice to enter the scoring lists. In actual fact, that goal at Norwich was the only one scored by him in League football.

Don't forget, of course, that much of Vic's career was spent at left-back and centre-half, positions from which goal-scoring chances are extremely remote.

After my opening match at Norwich, I stayed in Spurs' team, and a few weeks later, against Swansea Town, at Tottenham, I scored my first League goal.

Looking back, I cannot help feeling that no goal thrilled me as much as that first one. It was a header, and I recall how I had to dive forward to connect with the ball as it flashed over from the wing.

It seemed fitting to me, a young Welshman, that I should open my account against a team from Wales. And strangely enough, my next goal in League football was also against a Welsh team—Newport County.

We drew the match 1—1 at Somerton Park, but that goal is not on record. That may sound strange. The explanation is simple.

The game was played during the first week of season

1939-40. The war broke out on the following Sunday, League football stopped abruptly and all matches played during that opening week were expunged.

By touching on these reminiscences, I don't want to give undue emphasis to the scoring act. In football the scorers are less important than the score and no player should ever strive for personal glory in that sense.

For all that, I think there's a bigger thrill in scoring a goal than in preventing one. I must confess that the goals I have actually scored during my career have given me an extra personal kick.

Perhaps that's because I'm a defender, and goals have not come my way too often.

Now let me switch to another topic.

A lot has been said and written about the present standard of play in big football.

I realise that the players are not necessarily the best judges on this important subject, and that if gate figures are on the decrease, there must be a reason for it.

Some of the criticism I have heard has been fair. Some has been too sweeping. There is just one thing I would ask . . .

Before condemning the performance of any particular team or teams, give due consideration to the weather and ground conditions under which the match has been played.

I know the stock answer. Football is played under all conditions and the complete player should be able to adapt himself accordingly.

True, but often the conditions defy football at its best and those are the occasions when we can do no more than strive to put up a reasonable show.

A footballer's training is planned to enable him to perform on a normal surface for the simple reason that most grounds throughout the season are in a normal condition.

Moreover, you can train only on a normal pitch. The fields which are

Ted Ditchburn . . . they pulled his leg when he went on playing—unaware that most of the team had left the field !

only just playable cannot be used for this purpose.

If a pitch is waterlogged or snow-covered, it has to be left in the hands of the ground staff, who are often hard pressed to get it into shape in time for a game.

I have found from my own experience that the percentage of abnormal playing surfaces in the course of a season is surprisingly high. Adaptability is therefore an important part of a player's make-up.

When conditions are normal, by all means judge the players on the performance they have given. But when conditions are freakish, make full allowance for the handicaps under which they struggle.

One of the worst surfaces I have had to play on was in our third round Cup replay with Leeds United at Tottenham last season.

Shortly before the game was due to start a deluge swept the ground, flooding large areas around two of the corner-flags and leaving rippling pools in many places on the pitch.

Rain continued to lash down, and the whole field looked more like the seashore at low tide.

After a thirteen-minute hold-up, the referee decided to make a start and the ground staff were still trying to sweep the water away from one corner-flag after we had kicked-off.

Billy Rees, now with Leyton Orient, kept complaining about the weight of his case.

The ball played the queerest tricks, and a full-blooded kick often moved it no more than a few inches. Football under conditions like that is nothing more than a test of physical strength and endurance . . . skill counts for almost nothing.

Then there was the fifth round tie at Halifax the previous season. We played on a six-inch layer of snow, and were struggling as much to measure the pace of the ball at the end as when we started.

I recall, too, a third round tie at Huddersfield three seasons ago. Morning fog was dispersed by heavy rain, but the light was so bad that we could scarcely follow the flight of the ball.

Rain continued throughout the game and we were covered, head to foot, in mud. In fact, towards the end, Spurs' white shirts were almost indistinguishable from Huddersfield's blue and white stripes.

Strange that these outstanding memories of matches played under severe conditions all feature Cup-ties. Perhaps it's because the Cup-ties usually catch the worst of the winter weather.

The biggest laugh the weather ever gave me was when Nottingham Forest visited us in 1948. For seventeen minutes we played in normal light. Then clouds of fog began to billow in, smoke-like, through the opening between the Paxton-road and West Stands.

It was almost as if a machine were pumping the fog in and in a matter of minutes it spread over the entire field.

The match was abandoned, but Ted Ditchburn, our goalkeeper, who was the first player enveloped by this freak fog, remained between his posts, unaware of the referee's decision.

That gave Vic Buckingham, playing at centre-half that day, his cue for a joke at Ted's expense.

" How on earth did you come to let one through like that ? " he shouted as he raced up to Ted's shadowy figure.

" The ball hasn't passed me," protested indignant Ted, who was quite unaware that most of the players were by that time back in the dressing-room !

I've just space to finish with my favourite tour story.

The Welsh team were in Switzerland, and Billy Rees, who now plays for Leyton Orient, kept complaining, on the journey to Berne, about the weight of his case.

When we arrived at our hotel, Bill's first job was to examine his case. Inside, he found a weighty horse-shoe ! Alf Sherwood, the Cardiff left-back, was responsible, but the rest of us were also in the know.

Bill tried to get his own back by planting it in another player's baggage. But when the party moved off from Berne, it was back where it started—in Bill's case.

This time he raised not a whimper of complaint. I suppose you would call that a triumph of mind over matter . . . or perhaps Bill had just got used to the extra weight by then !

Eddie Baily (third from left) in action for Spurs against Burnley.

I've been lucky from the start

IF you've a good plan, stick to it. That's our motto at Tottenham, and we've every reason to believe we are right.

Under the guidance of Arthur Rowe, our manager, we have evolved a style that demands the maximum effort, by the whole team, to play pure, accurate football.

That means cultivation of the pass that allows for the least margin of error, and which must, therefore, produce greater accuracy.

It has been a joy to play under the tutelage of Arthur Rowe.

But, looking back, it seems I have been lucky from my earliest football days.

I seem always to have had the help and encouragement of people who like football only at its best.

Even as a Soccer-mad youngster at Detmold-road school, Clapton, I found myself in the hands of a purist.

Mr. Jones, our sports master, groomed me to use the ball even when I was only ten.

Kick-and-rush was frowned on. I was taught, from the start, that football should be played constructively.

From Detmold-road I moved to Mount Pleasant, another Clapton school. There my Soccer education continued under Mr. Eric Whittlestone, another teacher with scientific ideas about football.

With the right encouragement and grooming from Messrs. Jones and Whittlestone, I gained a place in the Hackney Boys' team, and also played for Middlesex.

Football had by this time become the most important thing in my life, and I couldn't have too much of it.

The nearest League club to my home was Clapton (now Leyton) Orient, who then played at the old Lea Bridge speedway.

I used to hang around with my autograph book, hoping to catch the players as they left the ground.

Ted Crawford, Dave Affleck and Charlie Hillam were among the Orient favourites of that time.

But watching the Orient could be a painful business in those days.

A gang of us used to wriggle in without paying and there were times when a clump round the ear from the gateman was our price of admission!

Sometimes I made the longer trip to Tottenham to see the Spurs.

Comparing Orient's old Lea Bridge ground with imposing White Hart-lane was like visiting a luxury cinema in London's West End after patronising a humble, back-street picture house.

When I went to Tottenham I watched the match from the boys' enclosure. I had to pay at White Hart-lane; unlike the Orient, Spurs had no holes in their fences!

Before I left school I was asked if I would join Tottenham Juniors, the young nursery team run by Spurs.

That was a thrill I shall never forget. Needless to say, I jumped at the chance.

"Dodger" Joyce, who looks after Spurs' junior players, was in charge of the team—so once more I was in good hands.

It was difficult to run a junior team in the early days of the war, but "Dodger" made a good job of it.

We played our home matches on the recreation ground in Lordship-lane, Tottenham, and in those days I carried my playing kit in a doctor's bag.

White, who was then a Chelsea full-back, and he suggested that I should call at Stamford Bridge on my next leave.

I did so and, on the strength of Alec's recommendation, Billy Birrell, who was then Chelsea's manager, signed me as an amateur, and played me in his reserves against Queen's Park Rangers on the following Saturday.

He told me to strip off for training and I ran round the Stamford Bridge pitch with the greyhounds, which were having their mid-week trials!

The dogs didn't bother me, however. With Chelsea willing to give me a game in their reserves, I felt I was already on a winner!

I didn't play in that match. On the day before the game I was in Tottenham and ran into Jimmy Anderson, Spurs' assistant-manager.

He had lost touch with me and nearly exploded when he heard I had signed a form for Chelsea.

Spurs telephoned Chelsea right away, everything was settled amicably and, from that day, I have been indisputably a Spurs player.

I have mentioned several people who have helped me along the Soccer trail. My greatest debt, however, is to Arthur Rowe, who thinks only in terms of pure football.

He has drilled us, as a team, to keep possession of the ball by means of accurate passing and intelligent positioning.

Not for us the chancy, long ball driven upfield in the hope of opponents making mistakes.

Naturally, Mr. Rowe is a firm believer in the methods that have won honours for the club in recent seasons.

I share that belief, and the rest of the team are solidly behind him in sticking to the style and methods that have paid dividends in the past.

Early last season we struck a bad spell and inevitably criticism came our way. Our answer has been to persist with the playing plan that has served us so well—that is: " make it accurate, make it quick."

We know its worth and have no intention of abandoning it simply because the ball may be running against us, or the team happens to have lost its touch for a match or two.

Of course, the boys "ribbed" me about that, asking if I was going to perform an operation.

I had my answer to that one—cutting a way through the opposing defence was the only operation that interested me.

After six months with Tottenham Juniors I moved to Finchley, but remained under Spurs' wing. I was still being encouraged to play football on the right lines, by Mr. Ernie Reeves, the Finchley team manager.

In 1944 I joined the Army and, after six weeks' training at Colchester, was posted to Edinburgh to join the 7/9th Battalion, Royal Scots.

I was a Cockney among Caledonians, but the influence of good football was still at work.

I had my first taste of Army football among Scotsmen and was delighted to find that most of them played the game the scientific way.

My Edinburgh posting also enabled me to watch Hearts and Hibernian. Both clubs have long had a reputation for good football—so again my education in Soccer matters was given a fillip.

When the war ended I was in Germany and, as a member of the British Army of the Rhine team, I joined the company of famous players like Billy Steel, Reg Lewis and Les Compton.

We were quartered together, and close and regular contact with them enabled me to share their ideas and views on football

—an invaluable aid to a young "unknown " with high ambitions.

While I was in Germany, I played for one of the local civilian clubs in Hanover.

They impressed me by their clever and accurate use of the ball and I felt honoured when I was invited to play for them.

It proved an important phase of my football development—one that stood me in good stead later on.

I'm often reminded of the fact that I once signed for Chelsea. This is how it happened.

During my Army service I met Alec

" When I asked him what Manchester was noted for he said Don Revie and Duncan Edwards."

Charles Buchan's
FOOTBALL
MONTHL

JUNE 1955

1'6

Overseas Price
Forces Overseas

BERT WILLIAMS of Wolves
saves from GEORGE ROBB of
Tottenham Hotspur

by TONY MARCHI
Tottenham Hotspur

THEY THREW ME OUT!

As a member of the Tottenham Hotspur playing staff I never have any difficulty in getting into their White Hart Lane ground. But once upon a time it was vastly different.

I OFTEN smile to myself nowadays when I enter our ground and think of the time when an attendant chased me.

I was a schoolboy at the time, and, like most of my friends in Edmonton, a keen Spurs supporter.

We used to pay ninepence to enter the ground, work our way into the enclosure, and then get into the main stand up a staircase.

One day we were caught by a steward, who took a dim view of our enterprise. Not only were we bundled out of the stand . . . we found ourselves right out in the street—with nothing to show for our ninepences!

There were three or four of us in the evicted party, and we had to club round to find sufficient ninepences to get into the ground again. Second time in, we gladly watched the match from our rightful place on the terraces.

It was war-time football at that time, and Spurs' ground was used alternately by their own team and Arsenal.

I was a regular visitor and no player impressed me more in those days than Jack Chisholm, the centre-half who left Spurs to play for Brentford and Sheffield United before moving on to Plymouth Argyle.

But I had another reason for being interested in the Spurs—my uncle, George Dorling, was playing for the club as a full-back.

Much of my early development was due to him. He spent hours in my grandmother's back garden at Edmonton, teaching me the know-how of football.

It was time well spent. I was only seven when I played in the junior side of Raynham Road School, Edmonton.

I was then an outside-right, and it wasn't easy to get into the team. The sports master would not give me a trial; he thought me too young for the school team.

Fortunately, one of the older boys spoke up for me and, under pressure, the sports master agreed to play me.

A trio of Tottenham talent . . . George Robb, Len Duquemin and Sonny Walters.

I scored three goals in my first match—and stayed in the team.

Things went well during my schooldays and eventually I found myself in the England Boys' team. My first international was against the Welsh Boys on Swansea Town's ground.

We won 3—1, and I got two of the goals. My wing partner that day was Brian Jackson, who now plays for Liverpool. By that time I had moved to the inside-right position.

My first away game for Spurs was on the Swansea ground. I played there in the Tottenham team that won promotion in 1950, a week after making my debut in a home match against Grimsby Town.

When I turned out for that match against Grimsby, Spurs had already made sure of the Second Division championship. But although I came through my debut satisfactorily, it was not a happy day for the team.

We lost 2—1, after Len Duquemin had given us the lead in the second-half.

In addition to those two games, I was in Spurs' first team for a full-scale friendly with Hibernian.

I was still an amateur, although old enough to have turned professional. The reason I wasn't a pro. was that I wanted to go with England's Youth team for the international knock-out competition in Austria that summer.

As soon as that tour was over I turned professional for Spurs. There was nothing wrong with that signing —but there was a time when I knew less about football regulations, and signed a form that led to complications.

The scout of another League club asked me to sign for his club and I did so.

I was still a schoolboy and when the news reached the ears of one of the schoolteachers running the Edmonton Boys' team he told me that unless the form was cancelled, I could not play in an English Shield match against Coventry Boys on Tottenham's ground that week.

Fortunately, it had not been sent away, and we were able to put things right.

Incidentally, we beat Coventry Boys 2-0 in that game, despite a brilliant performance by the visiting goalkeeper.

His name ? None other than Reg Matthews, who is now an England player, and the star goalkeeper of Coventry City.

After his display for Coventry Boys that day, it was no surprise to me when Matthews emerged as one of the finest goalkeepers in English football.

Before signing for Spurs, I was approached by Arsenal.

I went to Arsenal Stadium for an interview with Jack

Crayston, their assistant manager. The idea was that I should play for Chase of Chertsey, the Surrey club then used by Arsenal as a nursery.

This had little appeal for me. As my home was at Edmonton, it meant I would have a long journey for every match. So I turned the offer down.

I had previously played for Tottenham Juniors, Spurs' nursery team. Shortly after the Arsenal's approach—possibly because of it!—Spurs asked me to sign amateur forms.

When my turn for Army service came, I was lucky to find myself in good football company. I played in the 28th Battalion R.A.O.C. team that reached the Army Cup Final where it lost 2-3 to a Signals eleven.

In that team with me were Vic Keeble and Phil Gunter, who now play for Newcastle United and Portsmouth. The opposition included Alan Finney and Albert Quixall, the Sheffield Wednesday players—and other well-known professionals.

While I was in the Army, Arthur Rowe, who was then Spurs' manager, arranged to rush me by car from Aldershot to Southampton for a Football Combination match under floodlights.

Although I was a half-back, Mr. Rowe asked me to play at centre-forward that evening. I did so, and scored the only goal of the game!

Nothing remarkable in that, perhaps, **but that match was the first competitive game ever staged under floodlights in this country.**

That's why the goal has a special place in my Soccer memories.

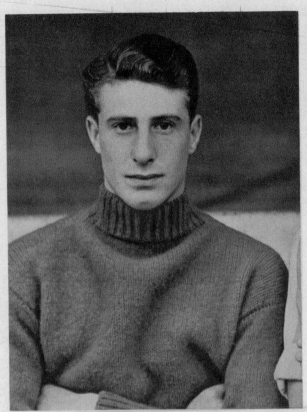

REG MATTHEWS . . . Coventry City's brilliant young goalkeeper, played against Marchi in a boys' match.

BRIAN JACKSON . . . of Liverpool, who was on the wing with Marchi in an England Boys' team.

JACK CHISHOLM . . . his play at centre-half for Spurs impressed the boy Marchi.

Above, all eyes are on the ball as Robb scores Tottenham Hotspur's second goal in the first Cup-tie against West Ham, at White Hart Lane. Left, a picture of despair is Gregory, West Ham goalkeeper, as he sees the ball go in from a Harmer penalty.

THESE SHOTS MADE THE CROWD ROAR

Below, a determined Tottenham raid is ended when Gregory leaps out and up to push the ball away.

Left, Gregory again leaps to foil a Tottenham rush. Below, another view of the Robb goal, with exultant Spurs throwing their arms up in glee—and Gregory looking as though he can't believe it.

Left, Reynolds, Spurs' goalkeeper, tips a shot from Dick over the bar. Above, six white-shirted Spurs are foiled by Gregory.

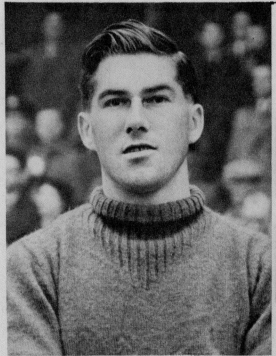

by RON REYNOLDS
Tottenham Hotspur

The greengrocer weighed me up

I WAS A FORWARD, BUT HE GOT ME A GOALKEEPER'S JOB

HAVE you ever heard of a young amateur inside-right being given a trial by a League club as a goalkeeper?

That is what happened to me.

I was not even a member of a club at the time.

After school I left home for five months to study draughtsmanship. That meant a break from football, but when I returned to my home, at Haslemere, I got an odd game or two with the local A.T.C. team, as an inside-right.

Then a local greengrocer—who had also been caretaker of the recreation ground on which I had played as a schoolboy—told me he had recommended me to Aldershot . . . as a goalkeeper.

His interest in me sprang from an incident that had seemed quite unimportant.

I had played in goal for my school team and I was in the habit of using exercise books as shin pads.

Once I left them behind in the goal-mouth after the match.

They were picked up by the caretaker—who often watched our matches—and as they bore my name and address, he brought them to my home.

In that way I became known to him and when, later, he heard that Aldershot were searching for young players, he decided I was worth a mention.

The fact that I had finished my schooldays as an inside-right didn't seem to matter.

I had attended Godalming Grammar School and in my last season finished as top goalscorer! But earlier, I had been keeping goal for the school.

I first went into goal when playing in the under-14 team. In a match our goalkeeper broke his wrist.

I was put in goal and two weeks later earned a place in that position in the school's senior team.

I was only 12, and the average age of the senior team was between 17 and 18.

I was so much smaller than the other boys that when the annual team photograph was taken, I had to sit in front, with the forwards—to be seen!

When I heard that Aldershot would be contacting me to play a trial as goalkeeper, I could scarcely believe it.

But in due course I received a letter from the club.

They gave me two trials before signing me on amateur forms.

My early matches for Aldershot stand out more clearly in my memory than lots of the games I have since played.

The first was for the reserves, against Luton, at Aldershot. We lost 3—1, but I gained a lot of encouragement from congratulations, after the match, from the Luton goalkeeper.

A week later I played against Southampton reserves. Then came my chance in the first team.

Broken wrists seem to have played a part in fashioning my football career.

I've told you how I was switched from inside-forward to goalkeeper in my school team, when the regular goalkeeper broke his wrist.

When I joined Aldershot, their senior goalkeeper was Flight/Sergeant Liddell, of the R.A.F. Well, he broke a wrist against Exeter City in a Wednesday match at Aldershot.

The following Saturday's match was at Bournemouth—that was in September, 1945, and I was still an amateur.

It was a match I shall never forget.

Every player likes to be prominent in his first big game. I was prominent enough—but in the wrong way.

I picked the ball out of the net seven times. We failed to get a goal.

It was certainly a tough baptism. We were four down at half-time, and the fourth goal has always stuck in my memory.

It was scored by Matt Busby, now the famous manager of Manchester United. Matt, then a Liverpool player, was "guesting" at inside-left for Bournemouth.

After that match, Matt played only once more—as a "guest" for Reading—before retiring from active football to take up his present post.

Although Matt scored only one of those seven, I had to be alert every time he played the ball. His midfield scheming did a lot of damage, and he laid on goals with fine regularity.

But in spite of the Bournemouth goal avalanche, I kept my place in Aldershot's team, and three months later turned professional for the club.

I spent five years with Aldershot and then moved to Spurs in a transfer that involved the exchange of left-winger Ken Flint.

Looking back over my career, I don't think I am being unfair to anyone when I single out Bill McCracken as the man who helped me most.

Bill, now scouting for Newcastle United, was then Aldershot's manager.

Although Bill had been a full-back, he realised the vital importance of angles to a goalkeeper.

And, as I was working as a draughtsman, he sensed that I was good material for any discussion on that aspect of the football art.

"If you could break out for Saturday's Cup game it would be a help!"

DANNY BLANCHFLOWER
Tottenham Hotspur and Ireland

TONY MARCHI
Tottenham Hotspur
and Lanerossi Vicenza

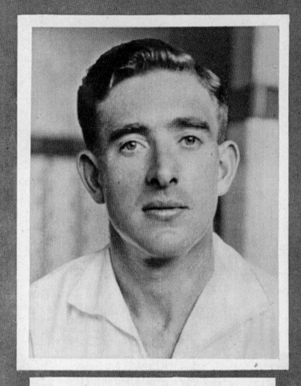

DANNY BLANCHFLOWER
Tottenham Hotspur

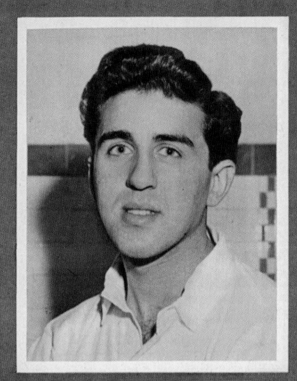

MICHAEL DULIN
Tottenham Hotspur

ALBERT STOKES
Tottenham Hotspur

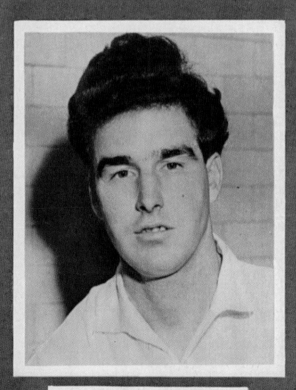

MAURICE NORMAN
Tottenham Hotspur

◀ September 1957 | 1956–57 Gift Book ▲

BOBBY SMITH
Tottenham Hotspur

Charles Buchan's
FOOTBALL
MONTHLY

1'6
Overseas Price 2/-
Forces Overseas 1/6

JANUARY
1957

TERRY MEDWIN
Tottenham Hotspur
and Wales

STAR-GAZING

with Scotty Hall

A new "Football Monthly" series in which this celebrated sports writer meets the MEN MILLIONS ADMIRE

No. 1: DANNY BLANCHFLOWER

of Tottenham Hotspur and Ireland

The Irish boy gift of the

I HAVE never forgiven, or forgotten, a certain Oxford don's definition of a football team—"Eleven oafs kicking merry hell out of a poor, defenceless ball." My dearest wish is one day to oppose this depressed don in public debate to one Robert Dennis Blanchflower, and that's Danny of Spurs and Ireland, as if you didn't know.

It'll be worth a lot to hear Danny boy's Shavian wit and Pepysian chuckle deflate the old prof. before finally persuading him that footballers, after all, aren't turnips.

If Danny Blanchflower entered politics, I'd vote for him, and, what's more, so would you, for he's got the darling gift o' the gab, and he's got the charm and the trick of making something off the peg look forty guineas' worth out of Savile Row, and he's got the smiling, puckered, honest face that's won more elections than all your preparatory backroom work.

"Sure I like to speak," says Danny, "for it's only by speaking that you find out what the other chap thinks. And it's only by listening to other opinions that

you learn something, isn't it now . . . ?" Sure and it is, Danny boy.

Now, I have never subscribed to the view, occasionally advanced by some of our sports pressmen, that the old-time player was a doltish, monosyllabic type to whom the higher reaches of thinking were uncharted territory.

You've only to look back to such free-thinkers and ready conversationalists as your own Charlie Buchan, dear old Joe Smith, or Scotland's unforgettables, Jimmy Brownlie and Alan Morton, to appreciate what a wobbly-angled view that is.

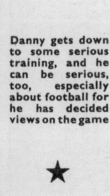

Danny gets down to some serious training, and he can be serious, too, especially about football for he has decided views on the game

★

But certainly it's a long, long time since any footballer has come upon the scene who is so quickly and competently prepared to talk about anything from a White Paper to the state of the going at Longchamps as our Danny boy.

"I say what I think," says Danny. "Sometimes it gets me into trouble. Arnold Bennett knew what he was talking about when he said, 'Truth, like the strong-smelling essence of violets, mustn't be sprinkled too freely.' But what's the use of saying something you don't believe ? Might as well keep your mouth shut. . . ."

Thank goodness for the gaiety—and "eedification," as Stoke's Bob McGrory used to say—of the Soccer nations that Danny doesn't keep his mouth shut for long.

Not even about football reporters— "And who do you think you are, miscalling the game that keeps you in a good job ? I like criticism. I know the game needs it. But this knock, knock, knock stuff churned out by some of the critics. It's a hammer they should be using, not a typewriter. . . ."

Here's Danny boy on how to win back Soccer's Missing Millions :

"We must make Soccer bright. Keep it bright. Remember that we're part and parcel of the entertainment business.

"Gone never to return are the old days when a bloke went to see a football match because he felt he had to go. Now other branches of entertainment want his patronage. And there's the lure of TV. But I'm not afraid of Soccer holding its own—and getting back some of the missing customers—if we remember to keep it BRIGHT.

"Put the accent on forward play. Tell

me, where's the thrill for the fan in watching a lot of dull, spoiling play? The fans want GOALS. Isn't the customer always right? So give the fans what they want —oodles of goals. . . ."

Is Danny equally frank about that reported £30,000 transfer fee which brought him to Spurs from Aston Villa? Every bit as frank.

It's his personal view that " nobody's worth all that money. It's the higgledy-piggledy state of the transfer market that brings about those fancy prices.

" Sometimes when a club fancies a player and hears that other clubs are interested, they'll pay the moon to get him. If I'm worth £30,000, *then Peter*

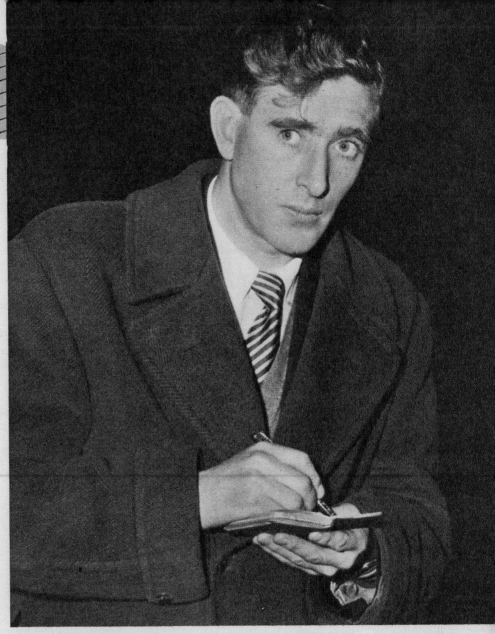

Never one to forget his fans, Danny is always ready to sign an autograph.

vith the gab

Doherty was worth half a million of anybody's money. . . ."

Mention Peter Doherty, and Danny's Irish eyes are smiling. " He was my hero," sighs Danny. " What a player, what a gentleman, and what a manager.

" Was Peter the best I've ever seen as a player of all the accomplishments? Sure and he was. The greatest of them all. . . ."

So I thought I'd tell Danny that this regard is not just one-sided. Tell him how the last time I spoke to Doherty, who's made such a roaring success of the Ireland team manager's job, he said to me: " Danny Blanchflower's influence on the Irish lads is terrific. His share in our recent international success is a big one. Every word Danny tells the lads they hang on to like gold. What a grand skipper and what a fine right-hand man he is to me. . . ."

I report to you that Danny blushed with a nice modesty. . . .

Maybe you've come on some of Danny's signed newspaper contributions and pardonably wondered if he knocks them together himself. He does. He's keen on the newspaper business, and he wants to learn all he can. His current bedside reading is William Hazlitt, and that, for me, is good enough to be going on with. . . .

There's a serious side, too, to Danny,

and here it is: " Soccer is a highly intelligent game. At its best, played by two really skilled sides, it is an intellectual treat.

" It is full of beautiful movements, ballet movements, if you like. It was never meant to be played in the air. Never meant to be a kick-and-rush affair, with smash-and-grab goals, and so on.

" Let's give the public real football. Let's get down to the business of playing constructive stuff, *precision Soccer, with the ball on the carpet.* It's a thousand times better to watch than all your mad, helter-skelter play that gets you nowhere very fast. . . ."

That's all from me, then, about Danny, except to say this. Woe betide that Oxford don who miscalled our football game should he ever find himself on the same public soap-box as Danny boy, that most articulate master of the football arts. . . .

" I've been sent off by better refs than you ! "

NEXT MONTH ┆ Scotty Hall goes STAR-GAZING at BILLY WRIGHT

DAVE MACKAY
Tottenham and
Scotland

No one lured me — I WANTED to go South

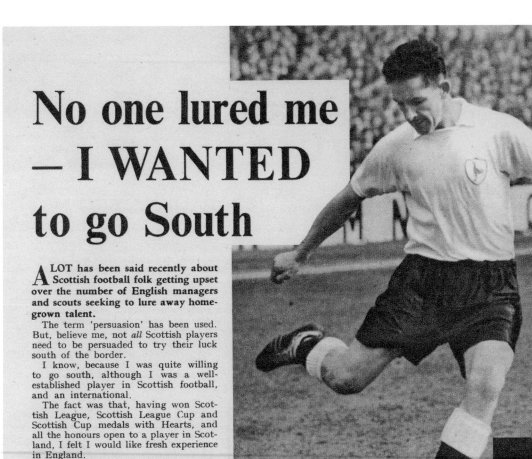

by DAVE MACKAY
Spurs and Scotland

A LOT has been said recently about Scottish football folk getting upset over the number of English managers and scouts seeking to lure away home-grown talent.

The term 'persuasion' has been used. But, believe me, not *all* Scottish players need to be persuaded to try their luck south of the border.

I know, because I was quite willing to go south, although I was a well-established player in Scottish football, and an international.

The fact was that, having won Scottish League, Scottish League Cup and Scottish Cup medals with Hearts, and all the honours open to a player in Scotland, I felt I would like fresh experience in England.

So I went to Spurs, and I have had no reason to regret it.

I have found the Spurs 'cosmopolitan' mixture—we have two Scots (myself and goalkeeper Bill Brown), three Welshmen, an Irishman and five Englishmen in the first team—a first-rate blend.

Like other Scots who move into English football, I found things a little strange at first.

The pace is quicker, yet although I am not particularly fast for a wing-half, I have been surprised at the ease with which I have settled down to the First Division tempo.

I know my tackling has been criticised, but I insist that I am a fair, if strong, tackler. I have always played that way, for I believe that the main job of a wing-half is to GET the ball.

That was the way in which I was brought up to play when I began my early football at Carrick Vale school, in Edinburgh.

I was a wing-half in those days, too, and won Scottish schoolboy honours against Ireland at Kilmarnock. I also had a trip to Wembley and went on as a substitute in the big schools international against England.

In those days most of the Edinburgh schoolboys team trained at Tynecastle Park, and that was my first playing connection with Hearts — although, of course, I had always been a supporter of Tommy Walker's club.

When I left school I signed Juvenile forms for Slateford Athletic, and then I moved into Junior circles with another well-known Edinburgh club, Newton Grange Star, with whom I had two happy seasons.

At 17 I signed for Hearts. Twelve months later I made my League debut against Clyde at left-half. I didn't do much in that game.

That was during the 1953-54 season, and later that winter I was given another chance in the first team—at right-half.

After that, I held my place and missed only occasional games, through injury or international calls, right up to the time of my move to Tottenham last spring.

I shan't readily forget my first full Scottish cap. It was against Spain, in Madrid, during the close season of 1956-57. What a tousing we got!

We went down 4—1 to the brilliant Spaniards who had Kopa, Di Stefano, Laddie Kubala and left-winger Gento in their star-studded line-up.

I was lucky enough to retain my international place after that downfall, and since then I have always been in the Scottish international squad, either in the team or as a reserve.

Last year, when Bobby Evans, of Celtic, was out through injury, I took over the captaincy for the game against Wales, at Cardiff—and marked the occasion by missing a penalty in the first minute!

We won 3—0, but I recall this game for reasons other than my penalty bloomer and first international as Scotland's captain.

All the Scottish forwards were drawn from English League clubs, and our inside-left, Dennis Law, of Huddersfield, was the youngest player ever to appear for Scotland.

Five Arsenal players were in the combined teams.

Wales had Terry Medwin—now a Spurs clubmate of mine—at centre-forward, although he did not like playing in this position and had, I believe, asked for a move from Swansea Town because they insisted on playing him there.

Phil Woosnam, of West Ham, also made his full international debut in that game — at outside-left — and he and Mel Charles were the outstanding players for Wales.

I was again appointed captain for the match with Ireland at Hampden Park the following month. We were held to a 2—2 draw after leading 2—0 soon after the start of the second half.

I had been right-half in those two games, with Tommy Docherty, of Arsenal, on the left-flank. For the game against England, at Wembley, however, Bobby Evans resumed as centre-half and captain. Docherty and I switched places.

I made my Spurs debut against Manchester City, at White Hart Lane last March, and shared in a 3—1 win, watched by one of the biggest League crowds I had played before since my 'golden days' with Hearts.

As you know, Spurs got off to a great start this season, and by the end of September were top of the League. Our best performances seem to have been saved for away games, and we had fine wins at West Bromwich, Manchester United and Newcastle and Manchester City.

We also won well at West Ham, but after breaking our winning 'duck' at White Hart Lane against Preston, we were well below form at Leicester the following week, and were lucky to get away with a draw.

This was one of my hardest games for Spurs, because in the second half I got a crack on the nose and played the rest of the game with blood staining the front of my white shirt.

There is a long way to go yet, but I'm hoping to collect an English League championship medal to add to the Scottish one I gained with Hearts.

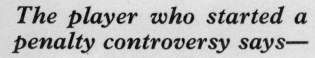

*The player who started a
penalty controversy says—*

Don't be sorry
for the goalie!

By TOMMY HARMER, Spurs' inside right

" **Y** OU should never fail with a penalty
kick." I hear it everywhere I go—
"Twelve yards away, a yawning goal, a
lonely goalkeeper. No doubt about it. A
certain goal."

I only wish it were so easy. I have been taking
penalties since I was 15 years old and I know by now
just how much luck and nerve is needed to score from
the spot.

The tension as you move up to place the ball is
tremendous at any time. When there is only five minutes
to go and victory is in the balance, it is almost un-
bearable.

And the poor kicker knows that he is on a hiding to
nothing. Most of the sympathy in this business goes to
the goalkeeper. I think it is misplaced. Nobody expects
him to save, and if he does he is a hero.

Confidence is the keynote to all spot kicking in any
class of football. The player must avoid getting flustered.
Above all he must know exactly what he is going to
do before he moves up to hit the ball. A moment of
indecision, a split-second change of mind and the chance
is lost.

When I was a boy playing on Hackney Marshes I
volunteered to be the penalty-taker. Even in those days
it was obvious I was never going to be the sort of
player who could blast ball, goalkeeper and all into the
back of the net. And that was the accepted method for
taking penalties in matches on those East London
marshes.

I decided, then, on the straight forward run-up to
the ball and the placed shot.

Except when I have been in teams where they have
a recognised penalty kicker, I have always tried to take

them. But once I graduated to the Spurs' reserves I
found that my straightforward method was not enough.
The goalkeepers were shrewder than they had been on
the Marshes. They began to note my mannerisms and
style, and I realised that if my penalties were going to
retain their surprise value I would have to vary my
method.

It was then that I hit upon the idea of running up to
the ball at right angles, pivoting on the left foot and
hitting the ball with my right.

The surprise value of this is obvious. Any goalkeeper
is liable to be disconcerted at the sight of a penalty-
kicker running up parallel to the goal.

I found, too, that by this method and with practice,
I could place the ball just inside the angle of the posts
on either side of the goal with reasonable accuracy.

I have since discovered, from looking at a photograph,
that Peter Doherty, the former international, now team
manager of Northern Ireland, sometimes took penalties
in this way, although I knew nothing about it at the
time I devised my method.

Towards the end of the 1956-57 season I found
grounds too treacherous for me to continue my angled
run-up. My left foot was slipping as I swivelled on it.
So my method changed again.

I went back to my straight run-up—but with a
difference. One or two goalkeepers, I had noticed, were
inclined to start moving before I hit the ball (not that I
blame them for that). It was only a split second, but if
they anticipated the direction correctly it was enough.

I decided to make a dummy pass at the ball before
hitting the real shot. If the goalkeeper was intending to
break the rules, this would show it.

Unhappily, this policy came home to roost last
season and I found myself the centre of controversy
after scoring from the spot against Newcastle. I was
accused of ungentlemanly conduct for making two
passes at the ball and having Ronnie Simpson diving
all over his goal before placing the real shot past him.

This problem of goalkeepers moving early is difficult
to solve. It is impossible for the referee, standing near
the penalty spot, to keep his eye on both ball and goalkeeper. I would suggest that the best position for him
is directly behind the net so that he can sight ball and
goalkeeper at the same time.

It would save a lot of argument.

▲ 1958–59 Gift Book | 1957–58 Gift Book ▶

TOMMY HARMER
Tottenham Hotspur

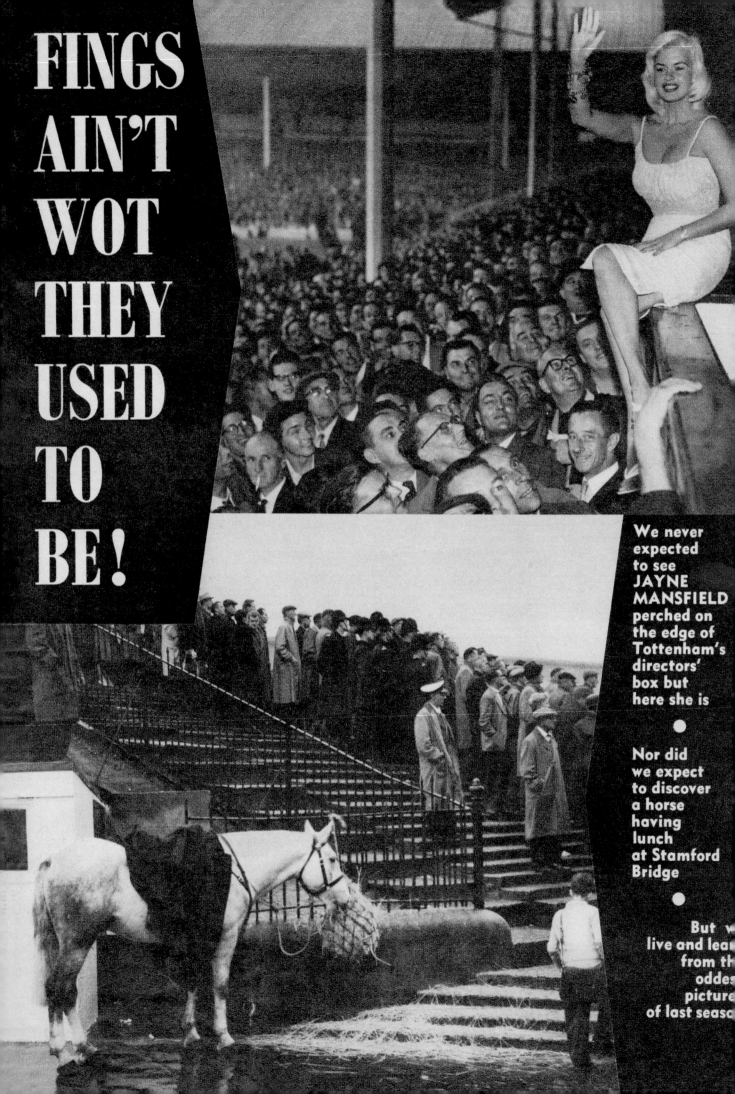

FINGS AIN'T WOT THEY USED TO BE!

We never expected to see JAYNE MANSFIELD perched on the edge of Tottenham's directors' box but here she is

●

Nor did we expect to discover a horse having lunch at Stamford Bridge

●

But y live and lear from th oddes picture of last seaso

I am really just a country boy up from the farm

says **MAURICE NORMAN**
Tottenham Hotspur

THEY say that if you play with good players long enough, you will become a good player yourself. Well, I like to think that has happened to me since I arrived at White Hart Lane as a very raw Third Division full-back, who even then thought he should be a centre-half.

Believe me, playing alongside such accomplished footballers as Danny Blanchflower, Tommy Harmer and Cliff Jones, not to mention our three great Scottish stars, Dave MacKay, John White and goalkeeper Bill Brown, has rubbed the rough edges off my style.

And it has also given me a new outlook at the art of centre-half play as the result of an experiment we tried during our club tour of Russia in the summer of 1959.

It was decided by our manager, Bill Nicholson, that instead of playing the orthodox centre-half game, I should stay deep *behind* my full-backs and allow our wing-halves to control the mid-field play entirely.

My task would be to pick up all the loose balls and generally cover the penalty area, making use of my height to head away the high centres and lobs from the opposing wingers.

This plan worked out very well in those Russian games and when we put it into practice in our League matches at the start of last season the success was maintained.

As you know, we made a good start and won many of our early points away from home. In some games, when we got well on top—and thanks to the fine play of Blanchflower and MacKay, we often did—I was able to temporarily abandon my deep-lying rôle and move up to support my forwards.

All this time, I felt my football ability was improving. In my Norwich days, I had been a bit of a "basher", at centre-half and at full-back.

With Spurs, I realised that there is far more to the centre-half job than just staying in the middle, "policing" the opposing centre-forward, or heading away anything down the middle.

Admittedly, I had to play a defensive rôle in our tactical plan, but I must stress that Tottenham are so much a ball-playing team that the centre-half job at White Hart Lane is anything but purely static.

After such an effort all through last winter it was a tremendous disappointment to us when we failed to win the League title.

But we cracked badly over Easter when we could not win our home games against Manchester City and Chelsea, and then we dropped another home point to lowly Luton.

That Manchester City game on Easter Saturday was a Soccer tragedy. You may remember that Cliff Jones shot home a penalty which was disallowed.

The referee ruled that as Cliff put the ball into the net after Bert Trautmann had parried his first attempt, the whistle had gone for half-time!

Had that score counted, I am convinced that we would have won. Those two points, and the one we let slip against Luton, made the vital difference between success and failure.

Like most tall centre-halves, I always find it harder to play against the small, nippy type of centre-forward. Len White, of Newcastle, always gives me a difficult time. And, of course, Tom Finney was the best centre-forward I ever played against.

What a loss the game has suffered by his retirement!

When I was a youngster at Norwich —I joined them from school in 1951— I learned much from Mr. Norman Lowe, who was then their manager. He took me in hand right away and the grand manner he had of imparting his experience to us youngsters was a revelation.

Another player who passed on many valuable tips was Reg Foulkes, the former Shrewsbury schoolboy international, who gave good service to Birmingham and Walsall before joining Norwich soon after the war.

In those days I tried to model my style on Billy Wright, but I seldom saw him in action and, in any case, he was physically very different from me.

I come from a little Norfolk village called Mulbarton and, before I joined the Norwich City ground staff—after winning Norfolk schoolboy and minor honours—I worked on a local farm.

Last summer I did what I have done for several years—I went back to work on the farm and so kept myself fully fit.

This farm work and the cricket I play with the village team of Breckon Ash, ensures that when I report back for pre-season training, I have none of the weight troubles that plague some big fellows like myself.

When I was at school I used to like playing at centre-forward, then I got a fancy for full-back. Now I have settled down at centre-half.

And I don't mind admitting that centre-half is the easiest job of the three —unless you are in a side that is repeatedly being over-run.

The full-back's job is the hardest. He has so much running and covering work to get through during the ninety minutes.

Spurs are quite a club to be with . . . but I must admit that I am a country boy at heart and it is the country that I love—particularly my little corner of Norfolk.

JOHN WHITE
Tottenham and Scotland

THIS is your life, Danny!

Danny Blanchflower, captain of Spurs, the Man Who Said No To TV's "This Is Your Life", is rooted on the goalline as he sees the ball hit the back of his net—put there by Jimmy Walsh (No. 8), of Leicester City. It was a slice of real Soccer life for Danny, and an unpleasant one, for it cost Spurs their unbeaten home record.

Charles Buchan's
FOOTBALL
MONTHLY

JUNE 1961

1/6
Overseas price 2/-
Forces overseas 1/6

STARS OF TOTTENHAM HOTSPUR

The Greatest Soccer
Magazine in the World

IT is the footballing fashion of the season to be a Tottenham supporter. Especially in North London where Spurs fans have never had it so good, nor given their lungs such an airing.

With good cause, of course! England's top club team of the year have packed in the fans, home and away, as no post-war side has yet done—not even Manchester United in their pre-Munich glory days.

Listening to the expectant hum of the White Hart Lane terrace types before kick-off time must be a nerve-wracking experience for the visiting side.

Atmosphere like this can do much toward wrecking the morale of a team before they even kick a ball on the Spurs' pitch.

Conveniently next door to White Hart Lane is the original "White Hart", whose boundary walls were there when Tottenham Hotspur built their famous ground at the back. This is the focal point of pre-match chatter, with no elbow room for your pint after mid-day.

Here, publican Bob Halbroek reckons to serve upwards of 2,000 customers in a couple of hectic hours on match days. At 5.30 many of them are back again, especially if the Spurs have had a good win.

Here, I found Lew Foles, Isaac "Toffee" Lester and Maurice Sofier, representing two generations of Spurs supporters.

Foles and Lester, the latter a dead "ringer" for film actor Jeff Chandler, have been watching the "Lillywhites" since the first world war. Both reckon the 1921 Cup-winning side a better one than the present combination.

Sofier, who goes to almost every away game and sees his heroes at least 30 times in a season, wouldn't know ... he started to watch the Spurs only in 1947.

He remembers Les Medley and George Robb, before little Terry Dyson,

but not Jimmy Dimmock, rated by Messrs. Foles and Lester as the greatest-ever winger.

All three have season tickets but deplore the Cup ticket ramp alleged to centre around the club. "We have never objected to players making a bit on the side through selling tickets, but now they are to get more pay they shouldn't need to do it in future," they told me.

Isaac Lester watches games in comfort now. But as a twelve-year-old, in 1919, he recalls being trapped in the crush behind one goal and fainting during a Cup visit by Leicester Fosse.

In making comparisons between the Spurs of today; of the 1950's under Arthur Rowe ("a great manager, was Arthur"); and of the 1920's, I could get the trio to agree only on one thing—the 1961 half-back line is the best of all.

These three seem typical of the 700,000 or so fans who have passed through the White Hart Lane turnstiles this season.

Most of them live locally, but Spurs have regular supporters coming from as far away as Southend and Brighton.

Each match Saturday these fans pour into Tottenham's busy main streets in something like 8,000 cars and motor coaches. This in addition to the average 10,000 spectators who come in by train from Liverpool Street.

No wonder the High Road shop keepers, cafe owners and tobacconists have been reaping a golden harvest from the Spurs success story, as home and visiting fans turn into Saturday spendthrifts.

In addition to providing for thirsty fans, the "White Hart" also acts as

headquarters for the 2,500 strong Spurs' Supporters' Club, of which Mr. E. A. Jones is secretary and a tireless worker in the cause of ensuring that his members get fair ticket allocation for the big games.

"The club help us a lot, but we really should smash the ticket spivs," declared Mr. Jones. Backed by their Arsenal F.C. Supporters' Club friends, Spurs fans have enlisted the aid of M.P.s to try and make ticket racketeering illegal.

The Supporters' Club, who run their own magazine—the "Lillywhite"—can count on a faithful hard core of 800 or so. For each away trip, even as far north as Newcastle, there is always at least a coachload of Spurs fans, brandishing the navy blue and white favours.

Like most of the wealthy clubs, Spurs do not seek cash aid from their Supporters' Club. "But," says manager Bill Nicholson," we help *them* whenever we can. They are good supporters and they

SALAD DAYS AT WHITE HART LANE

do appreciate good football."

Contrary to popular belief in some quarters, Spurs and Arsenal fans are not continually at loggerheads. Many Soccer enthusiasts in this part of North London hold season tickets for Highbury AND White Hart Lane. Spurs have 6,000 season ticket holders on their books, with a waiting list of more than 500!

But whether they drive in by Mark IX Jaguar from Hendon, cram into a trolley bus from Cockfosters, or queue for a green White Hart Lane special from Manor House bus stop, these Spurs fans have seen the best football in Britain this winter, have cheered brilliant play from home side and opponents alike, in London's cheapest sporting entertainment.

Danny ... Dave ... Les ... Cliff ... these are the golden boys in white shirts whose names roll round the towering stands when the Spurs spark off another attacking gem and the goals thunder in.

THESE ARE TRULY SALAD DAYS AT WHITE HART LANE.

PETER MORRIS.

It had been a tough season, but now came the toughest part—dodging the congratulatory pats (sometimes heavy) on the head as Danny Blanchflower led his Team of the Century down the Royal Box stairs at Wembley.

This was it—the goal that took the Cup to White Hart Lane. It was scored by Terry Dyson (not in picture) and left Leicester goal-keeper Gordon Banks without any visible means of support.

The roar swelled round the Wembley bowl . . . Cliff Jones (No. 7) had scored the first goal for Spurs—they all thought. But he hadn't—it was judged off-side.

The Choice of Champions

TOTTENHAM HOTSPUR F.C.

UMBRO sportswear
in the 1961 F.A. Cup Final

Available from all leading sports outfitters

Humphreys Bros. Ltd. Umbro Works Wilmslow Cheshire

Danny Blanchflower, captain of Tottenham Hotspur, who, having scaled every peak in sight, has to seek fresh worlds to conquer. In a flick of magic the camera catches a moment of wonder for two small boys . . . and perhaps a moment of reflection on all our yesterdays and to-morrows by the Irishman who has become Soccer's Pedlar of Dreams . . .

DOUBLE FACTS

T OTTENHAM HOTSPUR are only the third club in the history of the game to win the Football League and F.A. Cup in the same season. Preston North End were the first, in 1889, and Aston Villa did it in 1897. Thus Spurs become the first club to bring it off this century.

★ ★ ★

It is Tottenham's third F.A. Cup triumph and first appearance in a Wembley Final. They first won the trophy in 1901 when they beat Sheffield United 3—1 at Bolton, after a 2—2 draw at Crystal Palace. In 1921, they beat Wolves 1—0 at Stamford Bridge. They have also appeared in seven semi-finals.

★ ★ ★

Tottenham won the League championship for the first time in 1950-51, after winning promotion from the Second Division in the previous season. In winning the 1960-61 title they totalled 66 points to equal Arsenal's record set up in 1931. Last season, they won more games (31) than any other club in the history of the First Division, and their total of 16 away wins is also a record for the competition. They began the season by winning eleven successive matches and won the title after 39 games.

★ ★ ★

Spurs also scored 115 goals, the most in their history. They used only 17 players to win the championship and four, Blanchflower, Henry, White and Allen, played in every game.

Two-and-a-half million spectators — a record number in British Soccer history to watch a club in Cup and League in any one season—saw Spurs gain their "double".

The seven F.A. Cup-ties were watched by 474,363 (average 67,766) and 42 League matches pulled in 2,037,671 (average 53,314 at home and 43,717 away).

★ ★ ★

Spurs by winning League and Cup, qualified to compete in the European League Champions Cup and European Cup-winners Cup. They will play in only the League champions' tournament. F.A. Cup-runners-up, Leicester City, were nominated by the F.A. to play in the Cup-winners' competition next winter. In the traditional F.A. Charity Shield game next season, between League and Cup winners, Spurs may play an F.A. XI.

A sight which hasn't been seen since 1897 —the League and F.A. Cup trophies in the hands of one captain. Here is Danny Blanchflower posing for Soccer history.

▲ July 1961

A White Hart "angel" becomes earthbound to protest at Polish and British Press criticism of Spurs' tactics in the first game with Gornik. The "angels" were a small group of Spurs fans.

September 20, 1961

A NIGHT TO REMEMBER

SEPT. 13—EUROPEAN CUP, FIRST LEG (KATOWICE)
Gornik Zabrze 4 (Norman o.g., Musialek, Wilczek, Pohl). Spurs 2 (Jones, Dyson).
SEPT. 20—SECOND LEG (TOTTENHAM)
Spurs 8 (Jones 3, Smith 2, White, Blanchflower, Dyson). Gornik Zabrze 1 (Pohl)
(Spurs won on agg. 10—5)

N OTHING quite like the night of September 20, 1961, has ever been known in English Soccer. It was the night when Spurs, English Cup-holders and League champions, justified their title and upheld the great sporting name of their club.

Just a week earlier, in the Polish mining town of Katowice, they had been sent packing by Gornik, a team of part-timers. And 90,000 jeering, derisive Poles, the Polish Press, and some of the home football writers, had questioned their tactics in defeat.

A tired Spurs side, not fully recovered from a 1,000-mile air journey, had shamed English watchers by trailing 4—0 to Gornik until the last 20 minutes when goals by Jones and Dyson raised hope for the return.

But with two players injured, the Gornik fans booed Spurs off the pitch.

For their injured stars, Kowalski and Musialek, Gornik brought in Gawlik and Olejnik at White Hart Lane. But this time the story was so different.

In a tense, tingling atmosphere such as no international ever held, the Spurs charged into their task of wiping out the Poles' two-goal advantage. Their very lives might have depended on the result. And

nothing could have stopped those smarting Spurs that night.

Backed by a continuous, almost frightening roar from 56,000 fans, they swept the Polish side out of the Cup with a tremendous opening burst. And when they had gained the edge on the aggregate score they settled down, dictatorially, at their own pace, to subdue and crush their rivals.

Revenge was sweet and absolute. Facing a 5—1 score in the second half Gornik surrendered tamely, showing nothing like the fight of Spurs who had so splendidly come from behind.

Spurs: Brown; Baker, Henry; Blanchflower, Norman, Mackay; Jones, White, Smith, Allen, Dyson. Gornik: Kostka; Franosz, Alszowka; Gawlik, Oslizlo, Olejnik; Florenski, Pohl, Jankowski, Wilczek, Lentner.

▲ November 1961 | 1961-62 Gift Book ▶

ots . . . boots . . . boots!
d in them Spurs have
arched to glory. Here
trainer Cecil Poynton
checking over.

Behind the scenes with...

steam locomotive of the old London North
astern line proudly carried this name-
ate from 1937 to 1958. The plate
as presented to Spurs when the
gine was broken up.

TOTTENHAM HOTSPUR

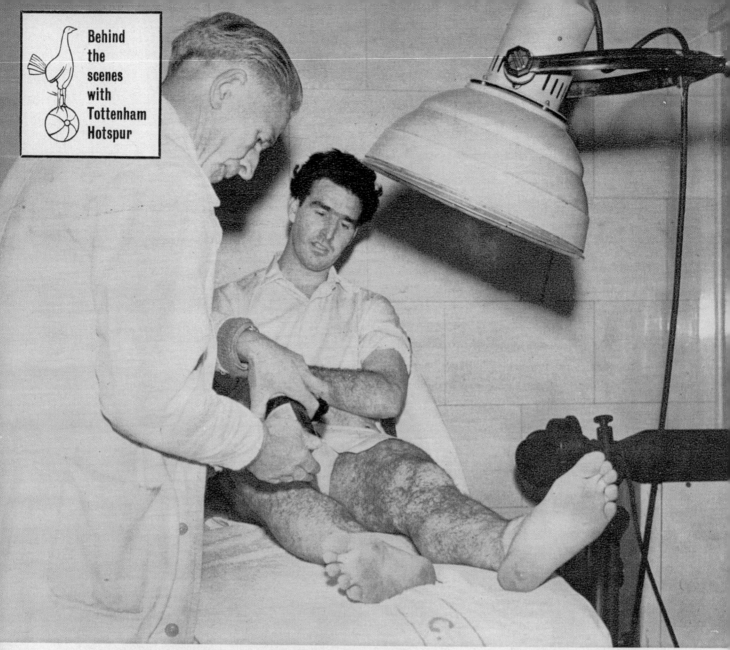

Trainer Poynton bandages the damaged thigh of Maurice Norman.

Cliff Jones, Terry Dyson, Maurice Norman and Bill Brown limber up.

Bobby Smith goes it alone.

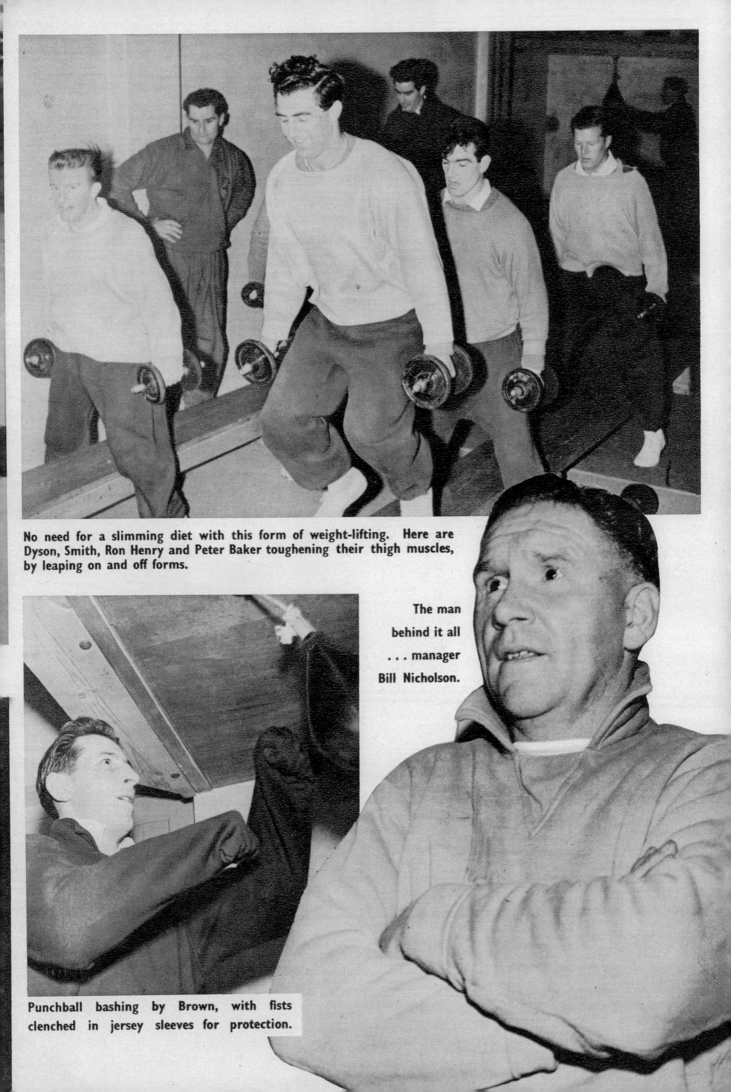

No need for a slimming diet with this form of weight-lifting. Here are Dyson, Smith, Ron Henry and Peter Baker toughening their thigh muscles, by leaping on and off forms.

The man behind it all ... manager Bill Nicholson.

Punchball bashing by Brown, with fists clenched in jersey sleeves for protection.

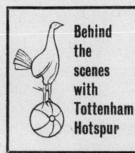

Behind the scenes with Tottenham Hotspur

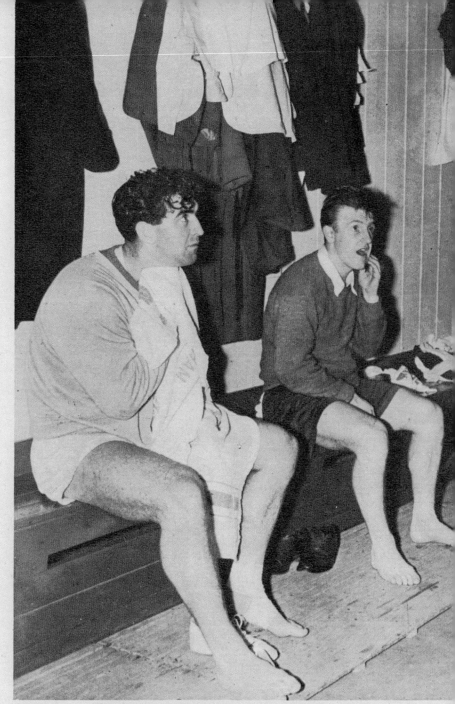

Nearly all over! Smith and Dyson have a well-earned rest.

A ballet pose by Brown during ball practice.

(Right): Underneath the rafters of the gymnasium, Norman goes up for the ball.

chat with trainer Poynton.

(Above): Skipping is not entirely girls' stuff. He-man Dave Mackay finds it useful.

(Below): A soaking in hot, soapy water—the reward for stiff training. And here are Norman, Les Allen, Mackay, Henry and Smith wallowing in it.

With Danny behind you you can't go far wrong...

says
CLIFF JONES
Tottenham
Hotspur
and Wales

THE winger is playing an increasingly important role in modern football and that was brought home to me in the 1960-61 season when I was switched from outside-left, my natural position, to the opposite flank.

At the time, there was a lot of argument about it. People said my most effective place was on the left, and that I should have been retained there. After all, they said, I had always played for Wales on the left.

From my viewpoint, the main advantage of playing on the left was that I could come inside my full-back on my right foot and bear in on goal *directly* because I am stronger on my right foot than on my left.

When manager Bill Nicholson switched me early in the 1960-61 season, I was, at first, all at sea. Injuries did not help, but eventually I settled down.

I then began to appreciate the advantages that came my way on the right. For one thing, I had Danny Blanchflower behind me and with the wonderful service this great wing-half offers his winger, one can't go wrong.

When on the left-wing, I had been considered an individual player and had not always had the same amount of backing-up from my colleagues as I got when I went to the right.

Once I had recovered the knack of judging my "blind-side" running on the right, and had overcome the natural tendency to take the ball AWAY from goal and up to the bye-line when beating a full-back, I was able to play my full part in the high-scoring Tottenham attack.

I found more opportunities to move into the middle, too. The way we were playing at White Hart Lane made for "fluid" forward disposition, and I knew that when I went into the centre, someone would automatically be in my position. Usually, it was Bobby Smith or John White, although Terry Dyson and Les Allen would sometimes move there.

Talking of Terry Dyson . . . he was one of the reasons why I stayed on the right. Dyson had played so well on the left-wing when I was injured that he could hardly be dropped. And, when I returned to play outside-right, Terry seemed to get better and better.

The man who had to drop out, of course, was my fellow Welshman and former Swansea colleague, Terry Medwin.

Strangely, when we played England at Wembley in November, 1960, Terry was at outside-right for Wales and I was in my old position on the left. He and I couldn't do much to avert that rather convincing England victory then, but there is no doubt that wingers CAN win matches.

The winger usually has more room in which to operate, and once he has beaten his full-back he is able to draw other defenders out of position.

That can be the most important aspect of the winger's job. But he must always try to make the final pass count, and be equally alert to finish off a scoring move.

In my time at Tottenham, I have taken part in many memorable League and Cup games.

Among those I shall always recall was the fantastic 4-4 draw with Burnley in December, 1960. Burnley were the League champions; we were riding high at the top of the First Division and unbeaten at home.

We were 4-1 up at half-time yet Burnley pulled back to a 4-4 draw in one of the most thrilling and skilful games ever seen by White Hart Lane fans. Considering the conditions—heavy rain and mud—it was a remarkable match and one in which I am proud to have appeared.

Then there was our 13-2 F.A. Cup slaughter of Crewe in 1960, after they had held us to a draw on their own ground on the previous Saturday. Every time we shot we scored in that incredible replay!

There have been some superb displays by Tottenham over the past few years, but I rate our 5-1 win over Manchester United at Old Trafford, early in the 1959-60 season, as one of the most outstanding. That game had everything—good defensive play and brilliant finishing power. It was a real all-round effort.

For Wales, I best remember our World Cup matches in Sweden where we gave a wonderful fighting display and confounded all the critics by reaching the quarter-finals where the eventual world champions, Brazil, beat us by the only goal of the game.

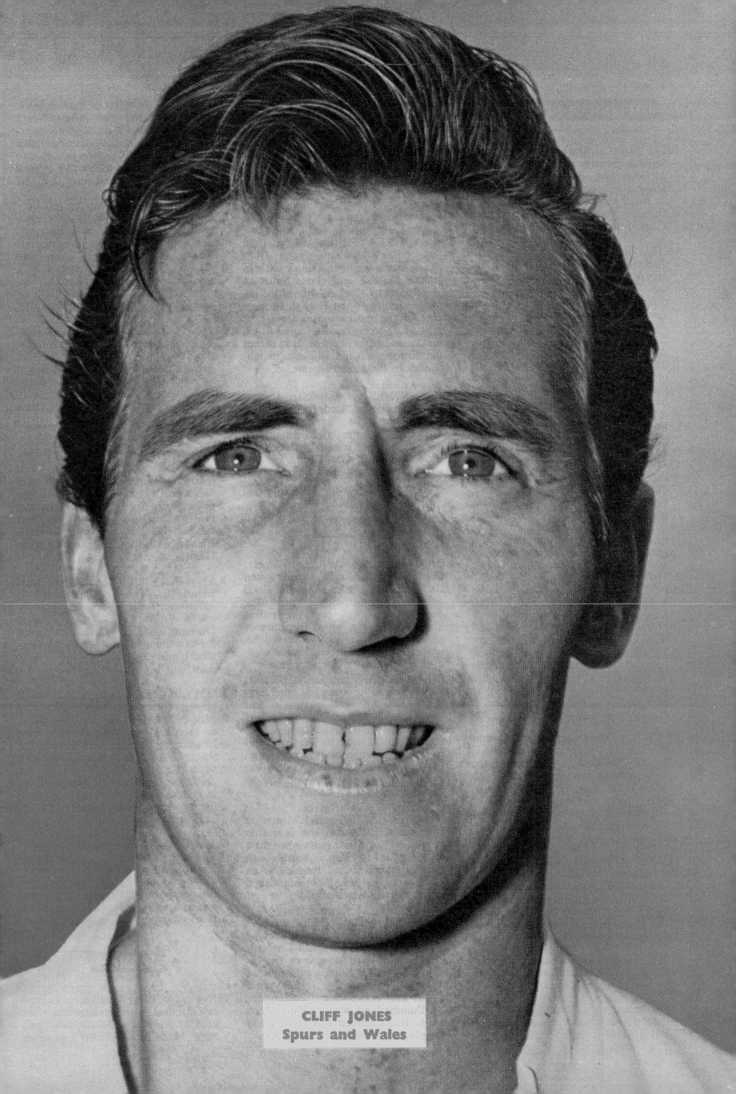

CLIFF JONES
Spurs and Wales

return of the prodigal

See that big smile on the face of Jimmy Greaves? He is happy . . . happy at exchanging Italy, the land of lira and sunshine, for Tottenham Hotspur and the dreary—but hospitable— streets of North London. Here he is training with Dave Mackay.

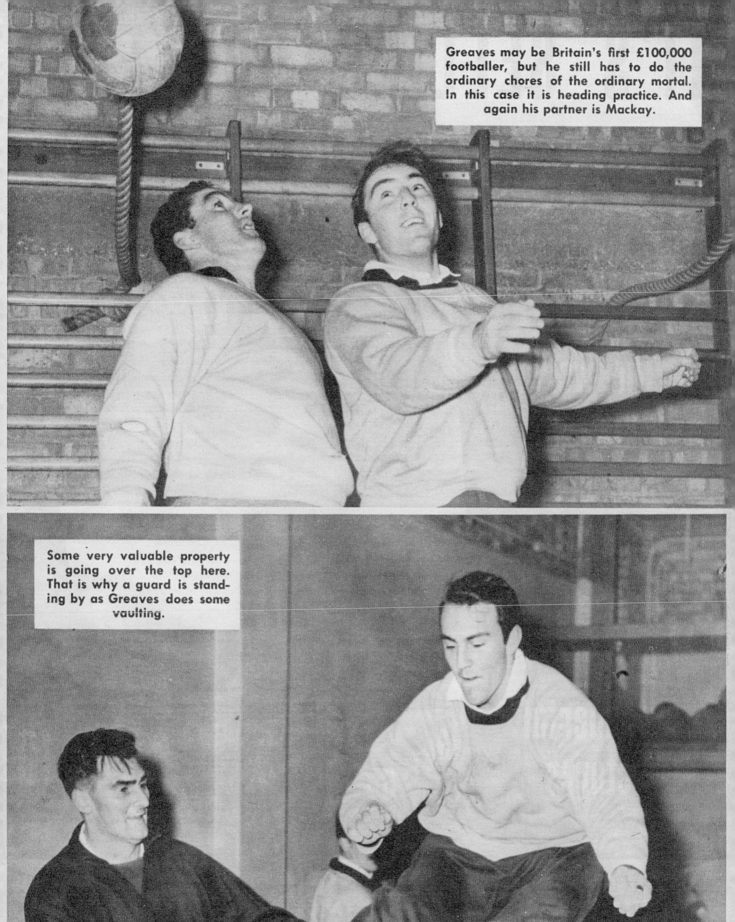

Greaves may be Britain's first £100,000 footballer, but he still has to do the ordinary chores of the ordinary mortal. In this case it is heading practice. And again his partner is Mackay.

Some very valuable property is going over the top here. That is why a guard is standing by as Greaves does some vaulting.

MAURICE NORMAN

RON HENRY

BILL BROWN

DAVE MACKAY

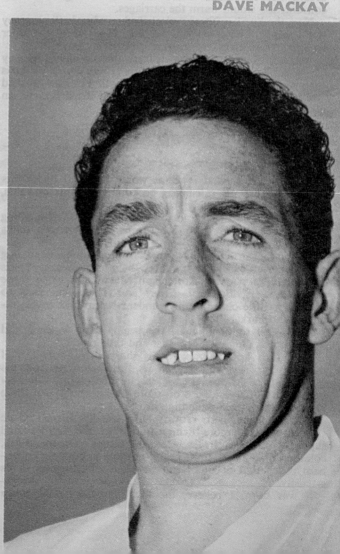

for services rendered

Club secretaries who would like to receive the same prompt service through their outfitters are invited to send in their names and clubs for a copy of the 1962 Umbrochure, which illustrates, in full colour, our complete range of winter sportswear. A copy will then be forwarded immediately on publication in mid-June.

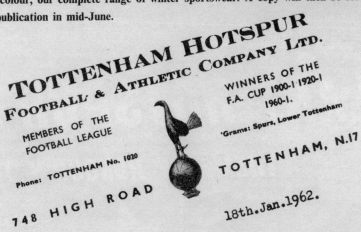

TOTTENHAM HOTSPUR
FOOTBALL & ATHLETIC COMPANY LTD.

MEMBERS OF THE FOOTBALL LEAGUE

WINNERS OF THE F.A. CUP 1900-1 1920-1 1960-1.

'Grams: Spurs, Lower Tottenham

Phone: TOTTENHAM No. 1020

748 HIGH ROAD TOTTENHAM, N.17

18th.Jan.1962.

J.Terris Esq.,
Umbro Works,
Wilmslow,
Cheshire.

Dear Mr Terris,

I feel I really ought to drop you a line to thank Umbro and those in particular who were responsible earlier in the month for the wonderfully efficient service they gave to my club.

It was a rush order, made on the monday by Mr Boyle our retailers, for two extra large football jerseys for our extra large centre half. These were delivered to me on the wednesday morning complete with club badge and number on each shirt, in plenty of time to make my centre half feel very comfortable in the evening F.A.Cup replay against Birmingham City, which as you know, we won.

It gives me great pleasure to receive such fine service and to thank those concerned.

Yours sincerely,
W. Nicholson
~~Manager.~~

UMBRO

The Choice of Champions

Humphreys Brothers Ltd.,
Umbro Works, Wilmslow, Cheshire

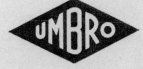

6

The proudest moment in the dreams of any Football League player—the moment when, as captain of his side, he receives the F.A. Cup from the Sovereign. Danny Blanchflower, seems more than usually delighted that his dream has come true.

Parade of triumph at Wembley by Brown, Greaves, Blanchflower, Mackay, White, Jones.

Blacklaw, the Burnley goal-keeper, went one way and the ball, aimed by Blanchflower, went the other way—into the net, from a penalty kick.

Consolation for Burnley. Robson surprises Brown and scores their only goal in the Final against Spurs.

HERO WORSHIP!

UP THE SPURS!

This was the night last winter when Spurs scored eight goals when knocking Gornik out of the European Cup. Bobby Smith got two—and this is what happened to him afterwards.

▲ 1962-63 Gift Book

Charles Buchan's
FOOTBALL
MONTHLY

SEPTEMBER 1962

The world's greatest Soccer magazine

2/-
Overseas price 2/6
Forces overseas 2/-

JOHN WHITE
Tottenham Hotspur
and Scotland

the game's the same . . .

Above, a scene at White Hart Lane. Thousands of the Tottenham faithful pack the terraces and stands to watch the ultra-sophisticated play of their favourites. This is football in the £100-a-week, Jaguar, class.

Not far away (see below) is a place where, for many top footballers, it all began—Hackney Marshes, a vast open space in East London where every Sunday 111 games are played on pitches so close to each other that spectators can watch several matches merely by turning their heads—and barking dogs are utterly confused by the number of balls to chase.

But whether at Tottenham or Old Trafford, in street, on waste land or marsh—the spirit of this great game is the same.

▲ January 1963

THE LABOUR EXCHANGE MAN GOT ME A TRIAL AT WEST HAM

(BUT I FLOPPED)

by LES ALLEN
Tottenham Hotspur

THE local Labour Exchange once got me a trial with West Ham! I wasn't out of work. I was about to leave school in Dagenham, and an official from the local employment office made the usual visit to ask us what sort of jobs we hoped to get.

"I want to be a pro. footballer," I told him. To my surprise the man from the labour exchange fixed things for me.

Not that it did me any good. The trial was held at Glebe-road, Dagenham, and I played against professionals.

I played in only one half and was told by Ted Fenton, then West Ham's manager, to come back two years later. Disappointed though I was, I couldn't blame him. I didn't put up much of a show.

So much for my early attempt to break into big football. My dream of getting a job on West Ham's ground staff gave way to the harsh reality of work as a storeman at the local car factory.

That is how I came to be playing for Briggs Minors at 15. Later I became an apprentice as a model maker, and after I had signed as a pro. for Chelsea, I carried on until I had finished my time.

I was in the Briggs Sports first team at 16. Briggs—now know as Ford United—were then in the Spartan League. In 1954 we reached the semi-final of the Amateur Cup. Looking back, I think that was my most thrilling Soccer experience.

For a raw 16-year-old it was an unforgettable moment when I ran out with the Briggs team on Newcastle's ground before a capacity crowd.

There must have been fifty to sixty thousand there that day. I had never played on a League ground before. And, after playing before gates of between two and three thousand, this was another world.

Briggs had beaten Bournemouth Gas, St. Albans, Bromley and Pegasus on the way to that semi-final. Then, against powerful Bishop Auckland, came the crash. We lost 5—1, and with that defeat went our chance of playing in the Amateur Final at Wembley.

Later that year I signed as a part-time pro. for Chelsea. But I have never lost touch with my old friends at Ford's, and I still take the occasional chance to watch the team play.

Before I signed for Chelsea, I had a letter from Spurs. I was invited to play a couple of matches in their "A" team. It was towards the end of the season, but it was not easy for me to get time off.

So nothing came of it, and more than five years passed before I landed at Tottenham in the transfer deal that took Johnny Brooks in the opposite direction.

I was only 17 when I made my League début for Chelsea. I had been playing at centre- and inside-forward, but was chosen at outside-right for my first League match. It was at Leeds, who had John Charles in their team. I came in for Eric Parsons, who was injured, and our forward line that day was, I believe, the youngest ever fielded in the First Division.

My partner was Peter Brabrook. Ron Tindall, Tony Nicholas and Frank Blunstone completed the line. The match ended in a goalless draw.

Chelsea were a good club, and I enjoyed the five years I was with them. But it was a great thing for me when I moved to Spurs.

There is an atmosphere at Tottenham that can never be captured at Stamford Bridge, but that is not the fault of Chelsea or their supporters. It is simply because the playing pitch at Chelsea is so far from the crowd, a player has a feeling of remoteness.

When I made my First Division début for Spurs against Newcastle, I played inside-left to Cliff Jones. Our attack included John White and Bobby Smith, and the half-back line was Danny Blanchflower, Maurice Norman and Dave Mackay.

With support like that I found my own job a lot easier.

Our double-winning season is, of course, the one that lives most vividly in my memory. It was wonderful to have a place in that history-making Spurs team.

For me the peak moment of that thrill-packed season was when the whistle sounded at the end of our semi-final victory over Burnley at Villa Park. The knowledge that we had reached Wembley gave us all a wonderful sense of achievement.

Beating Leicester in the Final climaxed that tremendous season. But even the thrills and excitement of Wembley did not surpass the magic of those dizzy moments at Villa Park when we knew we were through.

▲ May 1963

TOTTENHAM HOTSPUR : Standing—Baker, Allen, Norman, Brown, Henry, Smith, Mackay. Sitting—Medwin, Greaves, Blanchflower, White, Jones.

'He's a nice wee player,' they said (about me), 'but too small'

by
JOHN WHITE
Spurs and
Scotland

I SHALL never forget the day I was transferred from Falkirk to Spurs. It was a big enough thrill to join such a famous club, but at that time—October, 1959—I was not to know what brilliant successes lay ahead.

I was in the Army at Berwick at the time and Tommy Younger, then managing Falkirk, telephoned to tell me to meet him in Glasgow.

I knew it was about a transfer, but it was not until several hours later that Tommy told me I was booked for Tottenham.

Naturally, I was delighted. And if I had known that the next three seasons would produce a Cup and League double, a further F.A. Cup triumph and then the winning of the European Cup-winners' Cup, I doubt if my hand would have been steady enough to sign the forms!

Things could have worked out a lot differently. In fact, there was a time when it seemed that the bright lights of Soccer were not for me.

At school back home in Musselburgh, I was an outside-left. I was very small. The wing, it seemed, was the safest place for me.

I remember people saying . . . "he's a nice wee player, but too small." Praise perhaps . . . but not very encouraging.

By the time I left school I was taller, but still very slight. I joined the Prestonpans Y.M.C.A. team and moved to inside-forward. It seemed I had the stamina for that position in spite of lack of size.

When I was playing for Bonnyrigg Rose big clubs began to show an interest.

Johnny Love, then managing Walsall, happened to be staying at a nearby mining village. Someone must have put a word in for me. Anyway, Johnny turned up at my home at a time when I was actually training in the lobby.

"Is your brother in?" he asked.

That tells you how small I was. The Walsall manager mistook me for a younger brother!

Once that little misunderstanding was put right he made me a really good offer. But the prospect, coming out of the blue like that, scared me a bit. My mother was out and I told him I could do nothing until I had consulted her. I was told I would hear again a few weeks later. But nothing happened.

It is strange how much can hinge upon so little. If my mother had been at home that day, I may have become a Walsall player.

There have been other might-have-beens in my football life. Motherwell gave me a run in the reserves against Queen of the South. We won 2—1, and I scored the first goal.

Bobby Ancell, Motherwell's manager, was willing to take me on the ground staff at Fir Park. But as he was running only two teams he could not guarantee me a game each week.

Much as I wanted to get on in football I was unwilling to sit on the sidelines for even the odd week in three. I wanted a regular game, so I stayed with Bonnyrigg.

Then there were Middlesbrough. Bob Dennison, then the club manager, had me down on trial; Alan Stenhouse, who later signed for Motherwell, came with me.

We played in the reserves. Again I scored. Mr. Dennison seemed pleased with me, but again I was told I was very small.

I left Ayresome Park with instructions to do plenty of walking and skipping, and get a good quota of sleep. I heard nothing more from Middlesbrough.

Looking back, I know these experiences —discouraging though they were at the time—were conditioning me to the topsy-turvydom of football. Progress was proving difficult . . . but it meant that recognition was all the sweeter when it came.

Alloa gave me my first big chance. And then I was transferred to Falkirk.

My movement up the Soccer scale had been gradual, but climbing steadily through the grades must have helped me. No step was too steep at a time when I was developing my game.

I had moved from juvenile to junior class in Scotland; a harder grade. Then came the move to the Scottish Second Division, where I had to compete with players of keener Soccer intelligence.

It is a good thing for a player to come up through smaller clubs. He learns to appreciate the luxury of playing for a really famous club. The first thing I discovered on joining Spurs was how great it is to have first-class players around you.

Movement off the ball and creating space is an important part of an inside-forward's job. By playing in a top-class team my ability was sharpened.

Bill Nicholson, our manager, has told me this part of my play impressed him when he first watched me. At that time my play was instinctive, and I was not thinking deliberately of my movements.

Under his guidance, however, I have developed my "off-the-ball" play. He has made me realise how important it is.

So I now think about it. And if I am doing the wrong thing, I am quickly aware of it. This keeps me up to scratch.

In the old days in Scotland I was playing a type of game that came naturally to me. But often, I would lapse during a match because I was not conscious of the vital importance of taking up a correct position when a team-mate was playing the ball.

The set-up at Tottenham is out of this world. The training programme is carefully planned, and always interesting. And on a match day at White Hart Lane, with the vast crowd close to the pitch, the atmosphere is tremendous.

It is a great distinction to play for Spurs, and every member of the team gives all he has to retain that distinction.

There have been many wonderful moments in these past few seasons. But there are always fresh fields to conquer. My burning ambition is to help Spurs win the European Cup.

GLORY, GLORY HALLELUJAH !

Those whiter-than-white shirts look a bit grubby, but who cares? These jubilant Spurs don't. They had just marched on to victory in the European Cup Winners' Cup by beating Atletico of Madrid 5—1 in the Final at Rotterdam. Back row — Jimmy Greaves, Maurice Norman, Bill Brown, John White, Bobby Smith, Tony Marchi. Front row—Terry Dyson, Ron Henry, Danny Blanchflower, Peter Baker, Cliff Jones.

Left, beaten, baffled, bewildered, Madinabeytia, the Atletico goalkeeper, stretches for, and misses, a shot by Dyson (out of picture).

▲ July 1963 | April 1964 ▶

A very near miss!

A scramble . . . the thud of boot on ball . . . grunts . . . shouts . . . flying mud and slush! A goalmouth scene during the Spurs-Chelsea match. Eddie McCreadie, Chelsea full-back, goes sprawling as he saves a shot by Terry Dyson (white shirt, left).

PETER BAKER, Tottenham Hotspur

Now here's a jolly lot... a jolly, jolly lot!

Scene: White Hart Lane. Time: Last winter's big freeze. Occasion: Spurs v. Blackpool. Wonder if those policemen were thinking of their warm station, a big mug of hot tea—and a message to the sergeant... "Wish you were here!"

DANNY BLANCHFLOWER

CHARLES BUCHAN'S

FOOTBALL

MONTHLY

FEBRUARY, 1964

The
World's
Greatest
Soccer
Magazine

2/-
OVERSEAS PRICE 2/6
FORCES OVERSEAS
2/-

MMY GREAVES
rs and England

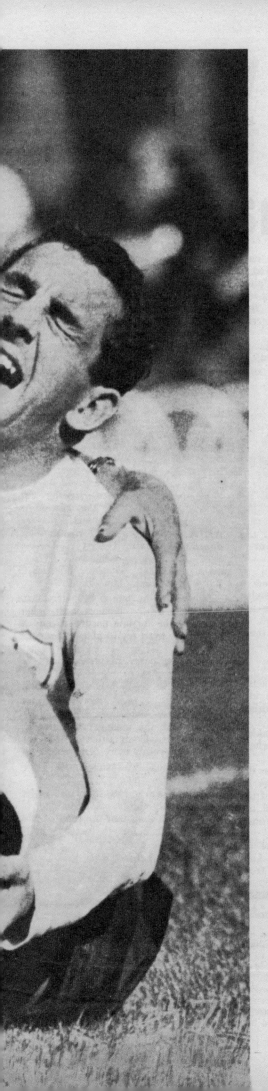

DAVE MACKAY

On the left is a picture of Dave Mackay, of Spurs and Scotland, going down at White Hart Lane with a broken left leg . . . you can almost feel the pain and hear the crack. It is the second time in nine months this has happened to Mackay—and this was another step to his come-back. It lasted twenty minutes. Below, he tells his story . . .

IT'S gone again . . . the pain . . . the crack . . . I've broken my left leg again! Others haven't realised it yet, but I know it—too well. It's the end of my fight to come-back. Now I've got to start all over again—all the waiting, the hoping, the sweating and slogging . . . the pain.

Look at the picture on the left. What I have said above were my thoughts when it was taken. The September sun was warm. I was on my way back to the top. I was confident of that.

I'd had half-a-dozen games and I was back at left-half for the first time since last December when I broke the leg for the first time at Old Trafford.

That night there was a 50,000 Manchester crowd, roaring their heads off for United against me and my Spurs chums in the Cup-Winners' Cup. But when this picture was snapped there were a bare couple of thousand to see our reserve game with Shrewsbury Town at White Hart Lane.

This was one of my few reserve games. I was enjoying it because, I thought, the long wait was nearly over and all the hard, lone training of a soulless summer was to prove worthwhile.

Long, long summer

It had been a long, long summer for me. I stayed at home when the family went for a holiday in Scotland. Holidays were a luxury I couldn't afford. They meant taking time—and time to me was priceless. So I stayed to lap White Hart Lane endlessly . . . pounding up and down the terraces. For company I had the echoes of my efforts.

Now my fight to come back is over—for a time. I am back where I started. And we had been playing just twenty minutes when this picture was taken!

These days I read a lot, I have plenty of visitors. It helps to soften the long waiting. The fans are great, too. They send letters from all over the place. Plenty from my own Scots people. It makes me feel I have done something worthwhile in the game.

I'm not a good football spectator; hearing the tidings at home is easier than being at a game. If the lads are up against it I want to be out there helping. There's no more useless feeling than that of being an onlooker.

Now I have to feel my way again. I want to get back, back to where I was . . . at the top. It's that or nothing for me. Frankie Blunstone, of Chelsea, cheered me with a grand letter —you know he suffered much the same injuries . . . and came back.

"If there's anybody who can do it, it's you, Dave," he wrote. I'm going to try darned hard to prove him right . . .

JIMMY GREAVES, *Spurs and England*

Bottoms up! Undignified, perhaps, but Bill Brown, of Spurs, has got what he wanted—the ball. So a Fulham raid was halted.

▲ March 1966 | June 1967 ▶

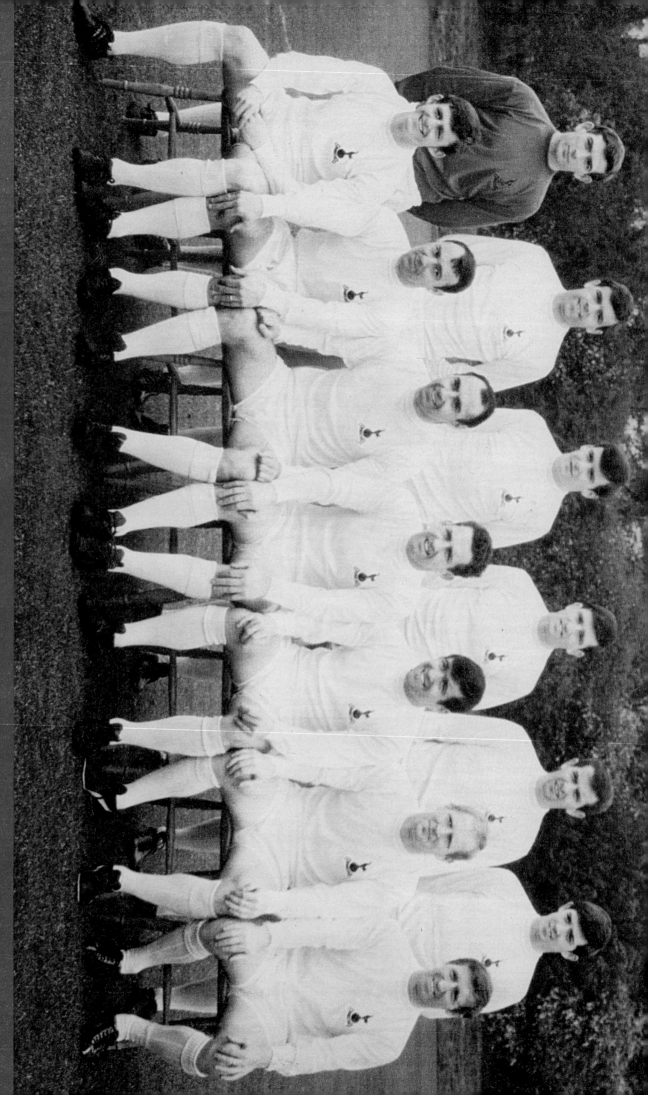

TOTTENHAM HOTSPUR
F.A. CUP WINNERS :

Back row: Jennings, England, Knowles, Clayton, Mullery, Kinnear.
Front row: Robertson, Greaves, Gilzean, Mackay, Venables, Saul, Jones.

SPURS

PAT JENNINGS

Goalkeeper: One of the best young goalkeepers in the game. Signed from Third Division Watford for £27,000 in June 1964 he took over from Bill Brown as Spurs regular goalkeeper. Started with Irish club Newry Town and turned pro. with Watford only a year before joining Spurs. Northern Ireland's first-choice goalkeeper.

JOE KINNEAR

Right-back: Born Dublin, he won an Eire cap against Turkey this season. Came to England as a seven year-old. Played for Watford Town Boys, Herts Boys and St. Albans City. Began as a wing half but when given a trial by Spurs was put in at right-back and they signed him on amateur forms. Signed pro. in February 1965, now 20, and got his chance when Phil Beal was injured.

CYRIL KNOWLES

Left-back: A fast-improving defender who has become a regular England Under-23 choice. Already rated a prospect for the 1970 World Cup. Spurs paid Middlesbrough £45,000 for him and it was money well spent. Also had spells with Manchester United and Wolves.

ALAN MULLERY

Right-half: Made the short trip across London from Fulham when the clubs agreed a £70,000 fee in March 1964. Bought as a replacement for Danny Blanchflower, Mullery has now settled as a basically defensive wing half. Has won full and Under-23 England caps.

MIKE ENGLAND

Centre-half: Spurs's most expensive capture. They paid Blackburn £100,000—a record for a centre-half—for him a day before the start of the season. A regular for Wales this six-footer dominates the defence but has also played centre forward.

DAVE MACKAY

Left-half: One of the great men of White Hart Lane. Broke his leg twice but has fought his way back and remains the driving force behind the team. Signed seven years ago for £30,000 from Hearts he is perhaps Spurs' finest buy. A member of Spurs' 1961 League-Cup double team he has two F.A. Cup Winners' medals and a European Cup Winners' Cup medal. Capped for Scotland at full and Under-23 levels.

JIMMY ROBERTSON

Outside-right: A fast clever winger signed for £25,000 from St. Mirren in May 1964. Born in Glasgow he has won full and Under-23 caps for Scotland. Started with Cowdenbeath as an amateur, also had trials for Celtic as a junior but moved on to St. Mirren.

JIMMY GREAVES

Inside-right: Perhaps football's greatest finisher. One of England's World Cup 22 but could not win a place in the final. Now fully recovered from jaundice he has regained his England place. He started his career with Chelsea and moved to Milan for £80,000; Spurs paid £99,999 to bring him back to England. Won a Cup winners' medal with Spurs in 1962.

ALAN GILZEAN

Centre-forward: Signed from Dundee for £72,500 in December 1964 he soon struck up an understanding with Greaves that has worried the best of defences. A tall graceful player he relies on craft and ball control rather than physical strength. Born in Perth he has been capped by Scotland.

TERRY VENABLES

Inside-left: Yet another of Spurs' expensive forwards, he cost £80,000 when they signed him from Chelsea in May 1966. He joined Chelsea's groundstaff as a wing half in 1958 and signed professional two years later. Capped by England at full, Under-23, amateur, youth and schoolboy levels.

FRANK SAUL

Outside-left: Versatile forward who has played in all the striking positions. A bustling energetic player who joined Spurs from school he can hold his own with the club's big-money signings. Born at Canvey Island he joined Spurs in 1958 aged 15 and signed professional on his 17th birthday. Has won a youth cap.

CLIFF JONES

Outside-left: Another member of the 1961 League-Cup double team. He has been troubled this season by injuries. Still tremendously fast he has a hard shot and is particularly dangerous in the air. Like his father, Ivor, and uncle, Bryn, he has been capped by Wales. Born in Swansea he was transferred from his home-town club to Spurs for £35,000 in 1958.

TERRY VENABLES

MIKE ENGLAND

PAT JENNINGS

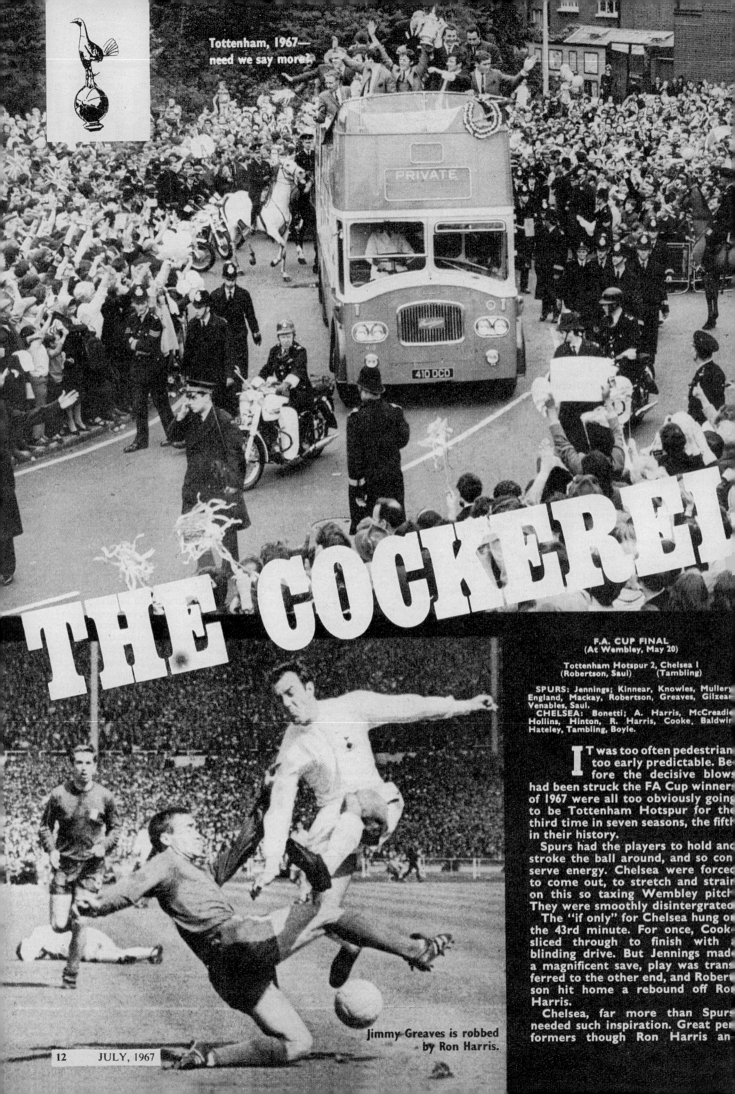

Tottenham, 1967—
need we say more?

PRIVATE

410 DCD

THE COCKEREL

Jimmy Greaves is robbed by Ron Harris.

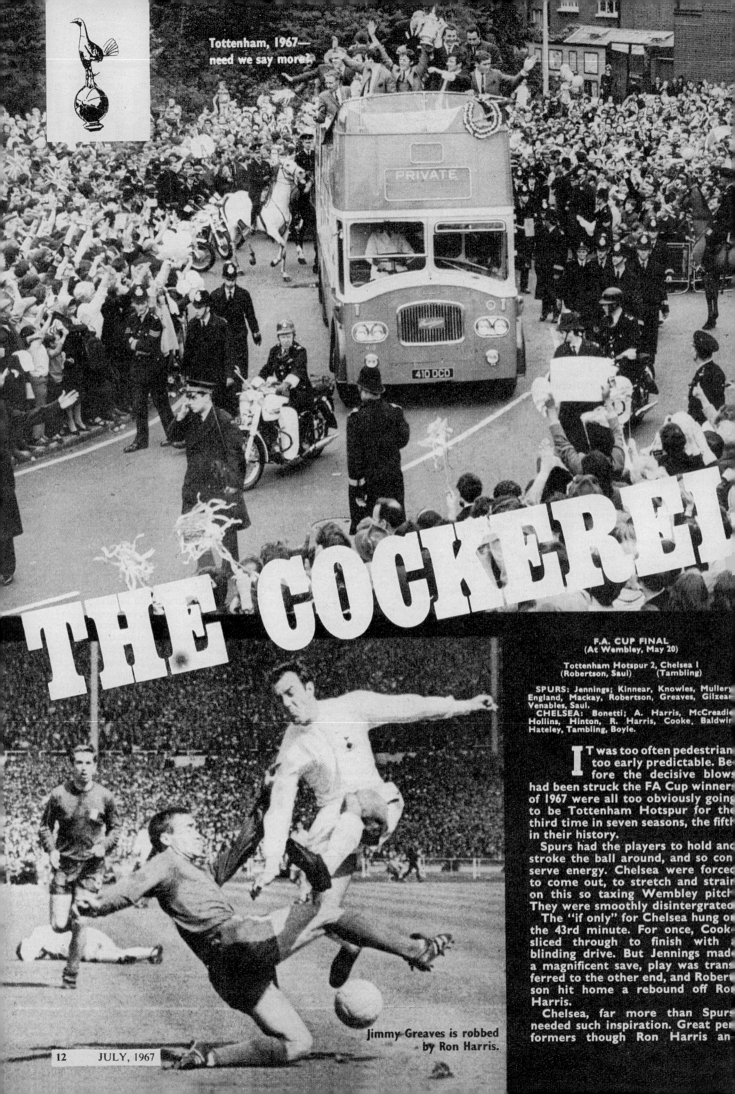

F.A. CUP FINAL
(At Wembley, May 20)

Tottenham Hotspur 2, Chelsea 1
(Robertson, Saul)   (Tambling)

SPURS: Jennings; Kinnear, Knowles, Mullery,
England, Mackay, Robertson, Greaves, Gilzean,
Venables, Saul.
CHELSEA: Bonetti; A. Harris, McCreadie,
Hollins, Hinton, R. Harris, Cooke, Baldwin,
Hateley, Tambling, Boyle.

IT was too often pedestrian,
too early predictable. Before the decisive blows
had been struck the FA Cup winners
of 1967 were all too obviously going
to be Tottenham Hotspur for the
third time in seven seasons, the fifth
in their history.

Spurs had the players to hold and
stroke the ball around, and so conserve energy. Chelsea were forced
to come out, to stretch and strain
on this so taxing Wembley pitch.
They were smoothly disintergrated.

The "if only" for Chelsea hung on
the 43rd minute. For once, Cooke
sliced through to finish with a
blinding drive. But Jennings made
a magnificent save, play was transferred to the other end, and Robertson hit home a rebound off Ron
Harris.

Chelsea, far more than Spurs,
needed such inspiration. Great per-
formers though Ron Harris and

CROWS!

The pinnacle of a
British footballer's life
—the Cup. And here is
Dave Mackay with it.

Hollins were throughout, the unusual Chelsea plan of committing Hinton to close-marking Gilzean instead of staying back to sweep up was shot to bits.

Hinton was never happy in the role, his unsteadiness, in place of the usual calm, affected the side.

Spurs cannily switched the usual roles of their wing-halves. Mackay wisely stayed put, Mullery was the marauding extra attacker. He did a great job. As did Robertson, Gilzean, Jennings, and the willing Saul—who fully deserved that second goal. But above them was the unruffled Kinnear.

Spurs' youngest Finalist, who took his chance like a veteran when Beal was lost through injury earlier in the season, had a dream game.

His way of making space to take a pass out of a pressed defence, or begin the many raids he set up on the right wing was the work of a matured, indeed, a highly creative professional.

Chelsea failed to gamble and throw in extra attackers until Saul had settled matters conclusively with his goal. Tambling's goal, from Jennings' only slip, five minutes from time, was but a reminder that Chelsea were not lacking in courage.

IF I kept a diary these are the entries which would make never-to-be-forgotten pages for as long as I play this game. And a long time afterwards . . .

Thursday, May 18: "Everything O.K., I'll be at Wembley after all! Our trainer, Cec Poynton had me try out the leg today. He was happy. How do you think I felt? Look out, Chelsea, here I come!

Friday, May 19: "Went with the team to Wembley. So far I've only ever walked on the famous turf, but it will be different tomorrow. There were only a couple of Press photographers about as I walked down the tunnel. Then it happened! I had a severe bout of 'shakes'. I couldn't stop it, and can't explain why it should come on just then.

"Hope it's not like this tomorrow.

Saturday, May 20: There's never been such a day as this! The Cup is ours! No nerves at all, I must have had them shaken out of me! The game went as we thought it would. It was just like a dream. Then the climb up to the Royal Box! Now I have a winners' medal. Words couldn't start to describe how I feel.

Sunday, May 21: "Our victory parade with the Cup was just fantastic. I've never seen anything like it before. It had me near to tears, all those great people turning out to greet us. The ride on top of that open top bus was a thrill I'll never forget.

Monday, May 22: "Reported with the England party at the Windsor Hotel, Lancaster Gate. Everything's happening at once . . . the lads meet Spain on Wednesday night and I'm on the party. First the Final, now this . . .

Tuesday, May 23: "Training with the England boys at Roehampton. I thought I was there for the ride. But when the team was announced in the afternoon I was in it! Marvellous! I was over the top about being nominated . . . now to play!

"John Hollins is in with me,

...WE ARE BIG

says
Alan Mullery

Spurs

his first cap. I'm so pleased after the great game he had for Chelsea in the Final. It's a grand consolation prize.

Wednesday, May 24: "Wembley again, the second time in five days. It's a habit I like! Really enjoyed the game against Spain, especially as the lads went to town in the second-half and earned a great win. The crowd was terrific, yelling us on all the way through."

Well, that's how it went, each and every one a day I shall never forget. And now there is

Europe ahead for Spurs and yours truly!

Imagine how I felt, that week leading up to the Final . . . i was one long sweat for me I've read and heard of othe players who had to sit on the Wembley touch-lines after help ing their club get there. The worst thing that could happer to a player, I thought. Bu when it really comes home to you . . .

My trouble was a knock o my right thigh in our last game against Sheffield United, befor we had to meet Chelsea.

I said a "knock". But I didn know what it was. That's wha worried me. Usually, you know how these things happen. Bu there was my leg stiffening up I couldn't recall how I had don it . . . I didn't know what t think. Dead worried, I was

It could be anything, thought, and began to hav horrible thoughts about having to bale out on the biggest day of my life.

But on the Wednesday I wa beginning to perk up a bit, th treatment I was getting seeme to be doing the trick. But had to miss our practice match Nobody was taking an chances, least of all me. It wa the end of a bad dream whe I was passed fit next day.

That bout of the "shakes on the Friday was all too rea I had never experienced any thing like it before. Yet on th day I felt terrific. The drive t Wembley, the crowds, th presentation, they all passe over me as if this was ju another game to be played As if the Final could ever b just that!

Perhaps it was confidence. I myself, in a great team, a grea bunch of blokes. We alway

BIG . . .

elt that we would win. Hadn't
ve gone 23 games on the trot
vithout being beaten? There
vas the fact, too, that we had
nore players with Wembley
xperience than Chelsea. I felt
hat would be important when
he chips were down. And so it
proved to be.

I put a lot of steam into the
hot I belted at Peter Bonetti,
nly for Ron Harris to block it.
t looked like a chance had
one . . . until Jimmy Robert-
on smacked home the re-
ound.

Right then and there I knew
where the Cup was headed for
. . 748 High Road, Totten-
am. Yes, White Hart Lane!
And I make no apologies for
alling on my face and bury-
ng it in that Wembley turf
t the end. I was so downright
vercome by everything.

I realised then that all the
hings which Bill Nicholson
ad said were open for me
vith Spurs, when he signed me
hree years ago, were starting
o come true. Bill had laid out
he prospects for me when sign-
ng me from Fulham.

Fulham had become my club
vhen, as a West London
chools player, some of the
lubs had started to take an
nterest in me.

Most of the London clubs
ad been along, but I had a
eeling they were not too sure.
But Fulham said they had a
lace for me. That was one
eason my father agreed I
hould join them.

There was another, equally
mportant, reason. Johnny
Haynes. Dad and I were great
dmirers of Johnny. My father
elt that such a player would
e an inspiration . . . and a
reat help. And so it turned
ut. I learned a tremendous

ALAN MULLERY . . . taking time out during training.

amount from Johnny.

Strange old game, this. My first League game for Fulham came when I was a raw kid, a couple of months past 17. It was against Leyton Orient. And the fellow I had to mark was playing his last game. His name? Eddie Baily, now assistant-manager to Bill Nicholson.

If I had been given a choice of joining clubs when Fulham were ready to let me go, then Spurs would have figured at the top of the list. As it was, they came for me . . .

A lot of "then and now" things went through my mind as I rode through the streets that incredible Sunday we brought the Cup for our supporters to see.

What followed that afternoon really shook me because about half-an-hour before we started out the streets were just about empty. Seeing this, I said to June, my wife: "It looks as if we shall have to wave at the people in the buses to attract their attention."

But when we got going . . . !

It was an amazing sight to see all those people. And a moving one. I saw men crying. Babies were held up to see the lads and the Cup. I'm not ashamed to say that it brought tears to my eyes.

Now I fully understand all that Bill Nicholson meant when I first met him and he set out for me what the future could be with a progressive club like the Spurs.

He explained it at our celebration dinner after the Final when he said that Spurs were nothing if they were not in Europe.

For this club of mine is a BIG club. They are out to win something. And that is the only outlook for the fellow who likes to regard himself as a professional.

Wish us good hunting. And all those other clubs which set out with us. Our British clubs have made them sit up in Europe these last few years . . .

And I want us to keep up the good work.

▲ May 1967

PETER MORRIS

spotlights
a man
who is
bound to
be in the
news again

Greaves in action
against Celtic

JIMMY GREAVES

How long can he stay on the goal standard?

THE more I think of Jimmy Greaves the more I marvel at the incredible consistency of the man and his goals over the years. And I wonder how much longer he can keep it up.

Greaves is pushing 28. He is still a young man although a grizzled old hand now alongside such as Peter Osgood, George Best and Rodney Marsh of the new generation of goalgetters.

Yet, in spite of all the close marking and the defensive barriers erected to shut him out, Greaves has scored goals with clockwork regularity over ten seasons with Chelsea and Spurs, broken only by his brief excursion into Italian football.

Ponder on it! Since season 1957-58, when he made his League debut for Chelsea as a teenager—and how long ago that seems now — Greaves has totalled 288 League goals for the two London clubs — an average of 22.8 a season!

For Spurs, alone, since November,

1961, when he returned from Italy, he has contributed 185 League and F.A. Cup goals, plus another seven in European Cup-Winners' Cup-ties.

In every season he has played in English football, Greaves has been his club's leading scorer. In 1962-63, he topped the country's scoring charts with 37. In 1960-61, his last season with Chelsea, he got 41 but Terry Bly scored 52 for Peterborough to head the national list.

In his first half-season with Spurs (1961-62), Greaves was the club's top scorer with 21 from 22 games; in 1965-66, when jaundice kept him out for a long spell and he managed only 15, he was still Spurs' highest marksman.

When he scored his 100th League goal three months short of his 21st birthday, Greaves became the youngest centurion; when he got his 200th in December, 1963, he was the same age as Dixie Dean when the old Everton leader notched up his double century—23 years and 290 days.

By the end of last season, Greaves

had been capped 57 times for England against home and foreign opposition. Often, he has lost favour with the national selectors—he even missed the World Cup Final against West Germany —but for all that, the figures tell us that the little fellow has tallied another 62 goals in international and other representative games. His 44 in full internationals puts him ahead of any-one else.

Even the two great Manchester United goal aces — Denis Law and Bobby Charlton—cannot quite match up to Greaves for neither has topped the national scoring lists in the Football League.

Greaves, in fact, is one of only three First Division forwards who have done it in the past ten years—Roger Hunt, of Liverpool, in 1961-62, and Ron Davies, of Southampton, last season, being the others.

If one took into account all the goals Greaves scored for Chelsea's junior and youth sides in his apprentice days, his total now would be a massive one.

As it is, he seems likely to pass Arthur Rowley's aggregate League scor-ing record of 434 goals. Maybe Greaves can also eclipse Jimmy McGrory's figure of 550 in first-class football which the old Celtic centre-forward set up over 16 years between 1922 and 1938.

Before this season's official start Greaves had opened his 1967-68 account with two typical goals against Celtic in that magnificent Hampden Park thriller.

Typical goals? What is a typical Greaves goal? It can be a thing of joy; a miracle of split second reaction; a classical offering of judgement and tim-ing; an explosion of spectacular and unexpected power.

It can be aimed from 25 yards out; hooked in from a few feet; jabbed home in a twinkling or chipped in with devilish cunning from off the bye-line.

Sometimes, Greaves has both started and finished the move; usually he has happened to be in the right place at the right time — from out of nowhere. Rarely has he missed the proverbial sitter; frequently he has scored off not a half but a quarter chance.

Anticipation has been his forte; cool-ness his ally in all the crucial seconds.

Only once in the history of the game has there perhaps been a Greaves pro-totype. They say it was Steve Bloomer who in his day and age exhibited many of the Greaves traits without half his sophistication. But like Greaves, he was a match winner.

The Soccer Gods have surely blessed Jimmy Greaves for they have granted him the power of scoring goals when it most mattered. Goals on his debut for Chelsea, Spurs and England for in-stance. What more could a footballer ask for than that?

But each season from now on, Greaves must lose a little of his speed. A fraction of his timing will go and he will not find it so easy to slip the tackle or evade a defender.

And his past reputation for snatching goals poses the dual problem of trouble to defences . . . and where will Spurs find his successor when the magic touch of the greatest goal scorer of this age fades and dies?

▲ October 1967

Star Strip

JOHN WHITE

FOOTBALL CAN ILL AFFORD TO LOSE MEN LIKE JOHN WHITE. PLAYERS OF HIS SKILL AND INTELLIGENCE ARE RARE, AND WHEN HE WAS KILLED IN JULY 1964 AT THE AGE OF 26, THE GAME WAS SO MUCH THE POORER....

...WHITE PLAYED 22 TIMES FOR SCOTLAND, AND IN HIS FIVE SEASONS AT TOTTENHAM HE WON TWO F.A. CUP WINNERS' MEDALS, A LEAGUE CHAMPIONSHIP MEDAL, AND WAS IN THE SIDE WHICH WON THE EUROPEAN CUP WINNERS' CUP IN 1963......

WHITE, CONFOUNDING ATHLETICO MADRID'S DEFENCE WITH HIS INTRICATE PATTERNS, PLAYED A HUGE PART IN 'SPURS' 5-1 VICTORY THAT NIGHT, THE FIRST SUCCESS FOR A BRITISH SIDE IN A EUROPEAN COMPETITION. IT WAS, TOO, THE LAST TRIUMPH OF THAT SUPER 'SPURS MACHINE OF THE EARLY 'SIXTIES.

IN OCTOBER 1959 SCOTLAND BEAT IRELAND QUITE COMFORTABLY IN BELFAST. MUCH CREDIT FOR THIS WAS DUE TO THE SEVERAL NEW FACES IN THE SIDE, AND TO YOUNG JOHN WHITE OF FALKIRK IN PARTICULAR...... HIS ARTISTRY WAS MAKING SEVERAL ENGLISH CLUBS SIT UP AND TAKE NOTICE. BUT BILL NICHOLSON WAS ALREADY MOVING....

WE'LL TAKE £20,000 THEN — WE DO NEED THE MONEY.

IT'S A DEAL....

IT WAS MORE THAN A DEAL—— IT WAS A BARGAIN. WHITE'S WORTH GREW, AND IN A SHORT TIME HE WAS WORTH FOUR TIMES THAT FIGURE. HE TOOK OVER THE MANTLE OF HARMER, BEING A BALL PLAYING INSIDE-FORWARD OF A SIMILAR VEIN....

NOW THE FINE, DOUBLE-WINNING COMBINATION WAS TOGETHER, AND EACH MAN KNEW HIS PART. BOBBY SMITH WAS ONE OF THE TWO STRIKERS....

...LEICESTER ARE FLAGGING NOW. WHITE IS MOVING EASILY DOWN THE CENTRE, AWAY FROM KEYWORTH AND APPLETON...TOWARDS THE LEFT....NO, IT'S A LONG ONE OUT TO SMITH, UNMARKED ON THE OTHER WING. OVER IT COMES, ON TO DYSON'S HEAD...IT'S IN AGAIN! NUMBER TWO FOR 'SPURS!

WHITE SCORED FEWER THAN THE OTHER FORWARDS, BUT HOW WE DEPENDED ON HIM. ONE FLASH OF HIS GENIUS, ONE LEAST EXPECTED PASS, ONE GLORIOUS IMPROVISATION COULD TURN A GAME..

...WHITE WAS THE QUIET, STUDIOUS TYPE WHO TOOK HIS SOCCER SERIOUSLY, ALWAYS THINKING, SCHEMING, CONCENTRATING.

R. BOND

WHAT GIVES THE GREATEST JOY TO ANY SCOTTISH FOOTBALLER? TO BE IN THE SIDE WHICH BEATS ENGLAND. THREE TIMES SCOTLAND DID THIS BETWEEN 1962 AND 1964, ESTABLISHING THEIR SUPERIORITY BEYOND QUESTION. THE IMPUDENCE OF LAW AND WHITE HAD MUCH TO DO WITH THIS.....

BECAUSE HE SEEMED TO FLIT AND FLICKER FROM NOWHERE INTO THE OPEN SPACES, JOHN WHITE BECAME KNOWN AS THE 'GHOST OF WHITE HART LANE'?..

IT WAS WHITE AGAIN, IN THE FINAL OF 1962, WHO LIFTED THE BALL ACROSS FOR SMITH TO PUT 'SPURS 2-1 UP AND FLATTEN BURNLEY'S HOPES..... SOME DIDN'T APPRECIATE WHITE. HE WAS A PLAYERS' PLAYER—— HE MADE IT SO EASY FOR OTHERS.

▲ 1967–68 Gift Book

CHARLES BUCHAN'S

FOOTBALL
MONTHLY

SPECIAL
200th
BIRTHDAY
ISSUE

APRIL 1968   THREE SHILLINGS,   USA 60 cents.

INSIDE

THE £1,000,000 TEAM
FABULOUS COLOUR SUPPLEMENT OF
BRITAIN'S MOST VALUABLE STARS

Tommy Baldwin (Chelsea)
clashes with Mike England
(Spurs)

The modern full-back has to work for his living

by CYRIL KNOWLES
Spurs

LEFT-BACK for Spurs against Newcastle on the Saturday . . . right-back for England against Russia on the Wednesday! That's how quickly events moved for me one week last December.

I must admit I had hardly expected my first full cap quite so swiftly as that. But Keith Newton, of Blackburn, originally chosen for the Russia match, had to drop out and I was called to take his place.

This was a really great game in which to make my debut—one of the best internationals seen at Wembley for a long while. And I can tell you that the players enjoyed it just as much as the crowd, despite the bitterly cold evening.

I wasn't quite sure how I would feel because I had to operate on the opposite flank to which I am accustomed for Spurs. And I found to my surprise that I had no opposing left-winger to mark for the Russians withdrew Malofeyev into a defensive position.

This meant I had the "freedom of the park" down the right flank and was able to carry the ball well into enemy territory before parting with it.

And I got a tremendous confidence booster in the first minute when I cleared a shot off the line with Gordon Banks beaten.

Of course, it helped a great deal having all that room to do everything. But that state of affairs didn't last as the Russians switched an extra man into their attack after half-time.

Nevertheless, I managed to play my full part in England's 2-2 draw—a result with which everyone was eventually satisfied—against a very fine Russian team.

In the England side, my briefing has been a little different from the job I do from match to match with Spurs.

Although it didn't quite work out that way against Russia because of their surprise move, I had instructions from England team manager, Sir Alf Ramsey, to stay tight on my winger. But I found myself with plenty of opportunity to

overlap—which the modern full-back can do so effectively.

In the Spurs side my role is rather more of a "sweeper-up" job. I'm expected to act as a general mid-field cover.

Manager Bill Nicholson is also keen on Joe Kinnear and myself overlapping whenever possible. But he insists that we get back in time if the move breaks down.

This is why the modern full-back must have plenty of speed . . . and he must be a good reader of the game as well.

I don't think the spectator always realises the amount of work a full-back has to get through.

Covering . . . tackling . . . "sweeping-up" . . . guarding the goalmouth in opposing pressure spells . . . dashing through on the overlap . . . I reckon a full-back in top football today covers as much ground in 90 minutes as an inside-forward.

I mentioned that when playing for England I am briefed in a somewhat different manner than before a Spurs game.

But this does not mean that Sir Alf

**BILLY NICHOLSON . . .
he likes me to overlap.**

Ramsey does not consider a player's job with his own League club. Quite the opposite. He is well aware of what each player is required to do, week-by-week, and does not make unrealistic demands.

I have found from my limited experience that in the England team there is at least this difference . . . there seems to be more time to play the ball—just as there is in the First Division compared with the Second.

I had my first experience of League football in the Second Division with Middlesbrough although I first had trials with two First Division clubs, Wolves and Manchester United—as a left-winger.

There is a world of difference between First and Second Division football—they're really two different games. There's much more of the long ball in the Second Division. In the First they generally play it much shorter.

But one thing remains constant—the problems posed for full-backs by wingers. And, of course, this applies down the scale to junior football.

For instance, with some wingers you can never seem to get in for a quick tackle—much as you would like to.

George Best is one of the wingers hardest to tackle. In fact, I would say it's almost impossible to deal with him in any conventional manner because he's such an unconventional player.

He has that knack of retaining the ball when by rights he should have lost it to you. A very difficult customer to tackle is George—he gets into his stride so quickly.

I find this so—and, indeed, against types of wingers similar to George, who is on the small side—because I am rather tall for a full-back and find it harder to turn very quickly because of my longer legs.

My ideal full-back is Ray Wilson, ideally built for the job, a quick and sharp tackler, a fine kicker of the ball at any angle and very speedy in recovery. Not for nothing was Ray Wilson a World Cup star.

And since I have always modelled my play on him, you can imagine the pleasure it gave me to play alongside him for England in my first international against Russia.

CECIL POYNTON, *head trainer of Spurs, says*

IN the 22 years I have been head trainer with Tottenham Hotspur I don't think I can recall a time when players were so prone to injuries as they are now. I'm not talking just about Spurs stars who have come under my care—but players in general.

I think one of the reasons, quite frankly, is that it's a job to persuade today's youngsters to wear shin pads.

I know that in my playing days we went to the other extreme by wrapping yards of bandaging round our legs as well as wearing thick and heavy pads. But to go into today's tough League games without any pads at all is asking for trouble. Highly-paid professionals should be forced to wear shin pads. It's true they won't prevent a broken leg but they do save some of the deep cuts and bruising on the shins which players collect so easily.

And in my experience, and it goes back virtually 47 years with one club—Spurs—I believe we are getting a lot more ankle injuries than we used to do.

This, I think, is caused by a combination of the low-cut Continental-type lightweight boot and lack of ankle protection.

Torn muscles are also a common injury. But this has always been the case since the game became faster and harder, as it has in the last decade.

THEY WERE TOUGHER

—and

well

padded

in the

old days

" Ron Burgess, one of the all-time greats at left-half "

▲ 1968–69 Gift Book

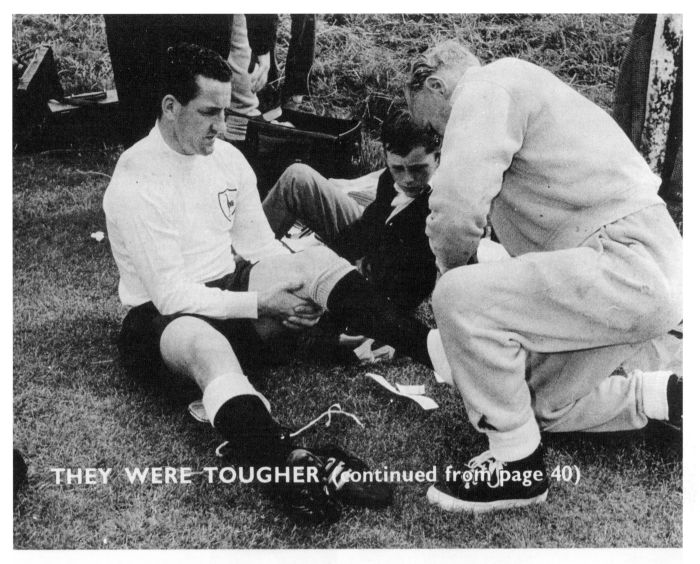

THEY WERE TOUGHER (continued from page 40)

Cecil Poynton—22 years head trainer with Spurs—attends to Dave Mackay.

Players train a lot harder today and see much more of the ball than ever we did in my playing days. As a result, injuries in training are more frequent although modern training is as different as chalk from cheese from the old days—and ten times as interesting.

Although today's professionals think for themselves more and, overall, are probably fitter and faster than my playing contemporaries I still think the old-timers were tougher individually.

Certainly they were not looked after so well as far as injury treatment comes into it—there was none of the expensive physiotherapy equipment available in my day—but they seemed to be able to shrug off injuries more easily than today's youngsters.

I've known players who could play while nursing injuries that would keep today's professionals out for a few weeks. In my time at White Hart Lane I can think of only four players who could do this—Bill Nicholson, the present manager, Bobby Smith, Dave Mackay and Jack Elkes, of an older generation.

The most serious injuries I have had to deal with in my time have all occurred in recent years—Mackay who twice broke a leg, Maurice Norman who also suffered a broken leg and Terry Medwin who eventually had to quit his League career.

Sometimes you can go two or three seasons without a club suffering any kind of serious injury and then you will get two in a row in which the treatment room is never empty. That's the way it goes!

Looking back now over my long time in the game it seems much more than a lifetime since I was playing for Brownhills Athletic, a junior team near Walsall.

From there I moved to Ton Pentre in South Wales and I followed Jimmy Seed to Tottenham as a centre-half.

I arrived at White Hart Lane in the summer of 1921 just after Spurs had won the F.A. Cup. The winning side was still playing together regularly and as a 17-year-old I had little chance of gaining a quick place.

My first League game, I recall, was against Birmingham at White Hart Lane and I was very impressed with the hefty Birmingham and England centre-forward, Joe Bradford.

Peter McWilliam was the first manager for whom I played at Spurs and I have now served under eight managers in my 47 years with the club although

Jimmy Dimmock, one of the best for Spurs.

Peter McWilliam had two spells at White Hart Lane in this time. I have also seen three secretaries come and go, up to the present one, Mr. Geoff Jones.

I was a member of the Spurs side relegated to the Second Division in 1928 and I finished my active career in 1936 as a wing-half.

Apart from a 12-month spell I had as player-manager at Ramsgate, the Southern League club, all the rest of my career has been with Spurs whom I have been proud to train in all their fabulous post-war triumphs.

I helped the club during the war years as a part-time trainer and was appointed assistant trainer, in 1945, to the late George Hardy.

A year later, when George died, I became head trainer and since then I have trained a Second Division championship team, two First Division championship sides (including the " double " team of 1961), three F.A. Cup-winning teams and a successful European Cup-winners' Cup eleven and also seen the club in four semi-finals and a European Cup Semi-final.

I have been in many parts of the world with Spurs and seen many of the world's stars in action. But of all the great players I have seen, I rate two Tottenham players the best in their positions—Jimmy Dimmock at outside-left and Ron Burgess at left-half, with almost 30 years spanning their different playing eras.

In recent years I have concentrated more on the treatment of injuries rather than coaching and training, as I used to do.

The time is coming when I, too, will have to leave full-time League football but I feel I'll always be a part of Spurs—for me the greatest club.

Left: Danny Blanchflower with the Football League trophy in 1961. Above: Mr. Peter McWilliam (centre) who signed Cecil Poynton in 1921.

February 1969 ▶

Youthful cheers for a White Hart Lane idol . . . silent appreciation . . . and (right) deep young thought, perhaps, on what's to come.

FOOTBALL MONTHLY

PAT JENNINGS
Tottenham Hotspur

JIMMY
GREAVES

Spurs

THE ONES YOU SEE...
THE ONES YOU DON'T!

YOU ASK HIM which is the greatest goal he's scored and he replies: "The next one." You ask him about his approach to a game of football and he replies: "I approach it to score goals. That's all." You compliment him on a goal that involved beating five players and screwing the ball in from an impossible angle and he replies: "Thanks —but the ones that bounce off my backside are just as important."

It's not that Jimmy Greaves—you must have guessed!—isn't very talkative. It's just that the little genius who seems to go on for ever, likes to do most of his talking with two of the most feared feet in football.

The above remarks aren't mere modesty; he really means that the *next* goal is the greatest; that goals are his business, and that's that; that a goal is a goal no matter how you get it in the net.

In a Spurs game early this season he received the ball 12 yards out, surrounded by opponents. The match was on television and you sensed that the commentator was waiting for the ball to be cleared —there was no excitement in his voice.

What happened next was a reporter's

Greaves the great goal-snatcher at work . . . a scoring position against Ipswich this season

nightmare, because reporters are supposed to describe goals. The only way to describe this one was to say that Greaves received the ball and then the opposing goalkeeper picked it out of the net.

It was sheer magic, yet Jimmy turned away with a slight shrug as if to say: "*Easy, isn't it?*"

But he doesn't mean to convey that impression. He once had the reputation among those who did not know him that he was a "big head." Not so. A big head could not be playing like Jimmy Greaves does after years of adulation.

He is 29 now and though Spurs are going through a rough patch, he shows no signs of fading from the scene. Defences are harder to penetrate, yet Greaves can still penetrate them with consummate ease. Or so it appears.

In fact, his genius, though natural, has to be worked at constantly. Those who decry his work rate fail to see that Greaves does not appear in scoring positions by accident. He is continually looking for the right space, waiting for the right time, snatching at the least opportunity.

He told me earlier this season when his manager Bill Nicholson tried him in midfield: "*I don't know if this will last, I'm really a scorer. That's what I enjoy, that's what I've always done best.*"

He was soon back in the front line!

If Greaves is at all complacent about his scoring feats, then there are statistics to excuse him. In League matches alone, with Chelsea and Spurs, he has scored around 350 goals. He had reached 100 before the age of 21. He scored 124 League goals in 197 appearances for Chelsea. And so on. . . .

But his career has not been without low points, or indeed controversial points. His spell in Italy with A.C. Milan—after leaving Chelsea—was not a success. He never really settled over there. Few have, though Gerry Hitchens and John Charles managed to make the transition successfully.

But Greaves is really a Londoner and it was no surprise when he returned to London in 1961. The move cost Spurs £99,999 and they have never made a better investment.

Yet it was Sir Alf Ramsey who took the stick three years when he omitted Greaves from England's World Cup Final side.

"*Madness*" they called it—but England won. There are still those who would love to see Greaves back in the white shirt of his country, but they have to make do with the white shirt of Spurs.

Stories of a row between Ramsey and Greaves are nonsense. Jimmy's statement that he no longer wanted to play for England arose simply because he and Ramsey stood for different viewpoints.

Greaves could not see why he should spend days—even weeks—with a group of players and then find he wasn't in the team. Regimentation is not his line— but he respects it.

And the respect is mutual. Ramsey, a fluid and superb player in the great Spurs push-and-run side of Arthur Rowe's heyday as manager, doubtless would like Greaves in his side.

But Ramsey's job is to win matches, not cater for his own personal whims. So Greaves is out. And always will be.

It is of no great importance now. Jimmy is living off the fruits of his genius—a packaging business, a sportswear business in partnership with Geoff Hurst (what irony; Hurst replaced Greaves in the World Cup), a splendid home at Brentwood—these are the rewards of top class professional football.

But Greaves hasn't gone into retirement, as every defender in the First Division continues to discover. His appetite for goals is still there and the public's appetite for watching him is as strong as ever.

And I must say that, for different reasons, I agree with Jim—a Greaves goal is something, however it's scored.

PETER BARNARD

PHIL BEAL

SPURS' MR. MODESTY

by Keith Fisher

TALK about a team like Tottenham and it's odds on the conversation will soon be centred around players like Alan Mullery, Pat Jennings and Martin Peters.

In a side flush with outstanding internationals, other names tend to be overlooked. Phil Beal, for example, is rarely in the headlines.

Yet few people will doubt if there is another defender in the First Division who is playing more consistently or more brilliantly.

Perhaps it was his unheralded arrival that cast for him a background role. It cost the club a paltry £10 signing-on fee when Beal changed his status in a Spurs jersey from amateur to professional.

Affable, quiet and unassuming, Beal still looks back in awe on the day he arrived on the

Beal . . . survived great shake-up

star-studded White Hart Lane scene in the summer of 1960. Says Beal: "I was only 15 and frightened stiff. There I was in the company of players like Danny Blanchflower, John White and Bill Brown. I was so nervous I nearly ran all the way home!"

In the early days Beal had a long uphill struggle in his fight for first-team recognition. It wasn't easy for a cost-nothing kid to make an impact in a side composed mainly of big-money signings and whose recent past contained the heady "glory, glory" days of The Double.

Beal — the longest serving player on the club's books though still only 25—has worn eight different jerseys at Tottenham yet has still made sure of a regular place.

He has faced up to the challenge offered by Cyril Knowles, Alan Mullery, Dave Mackay, Maurice Norman and Mike England . . . and still won through. He has been used as an orthodox full-back on either flank . . . a sweeper . . . a defensive wing-half . . . midfield organiser and an extra defender in a forward's shirt.

It is this versatility and his downright honest-to-goodness effort every time he sets foot on to the pitch which makes him so popular—even with those fickle fans in the stands of Tottenham's White Hart Lane.

Beal, born in Godstone, Surrey, was taken on to Tottenham's groundstaff as an amateur after being spotted playing for Surrey Schoolboys at The Valley by the late Harry Evans.

Even then Beal had a fight on his hands. Midway through his apprenticeship manager Bill Nicholson had doubts as to whether Beal would make the grade because of his 8 st. frame.

But there was nothing basically wrong that a few good steaks wouldn't put right and Nicholson soon realised that this likeable, modest young man, whose only international honour is an England Youth cap, was worth a place among the stars.

Since his debut against Aston Villa at Villa Park in September 1963 Beal has made over 200 League appearances. In that time the "Modest One" of White Hart Lane has had few bad games. And with his permanency at left-half has come a real confidence in his play.

Perhaps the greatest tribute to Beal came when he survived the biggest shake-up in the club's history after Spurs' dismissal from the F.A. Cup at the hands of struggling London neighbours Crystal Palace last season.

Included among Bill Nicholson's purge then were big-money signings Jimmy Greaves, Alan Gilzean and Cyril Knowles, who cost a staggering £217,000 altogether, plus Eire international full-back Joe Kinnear.

That Beal remained was due as much to the club's appreciation of his character and dedication as to their new intensified drive for youth under the able Pat Welton, who had been a great success with the England Youth team.

Yet talk to Beal about his part in the Spurs revival this season and in typical fashion he shuns the limelight and points to the success of the fellows around him.

Says Beal: "Really the whole side is playing with so much confidence. Take Martin Chivers up front. To see him play nowadays you wouldn't believe the worries he's had since he joined us from Southampton—a bad knee injury and loss of form—but he's been a revelation this season.

"Then take the midfield trio of Martin Peters, Alan Mullery and young Stevie Perryman, which is surely one of the best in the game.

"I suppose my big break came when Dave Mackay was sold to Derby a few seasons back. Although the gap he created gave me my chance for a settled place in the side I felt really sad when he left. It was a privilege for me to have played with him. Dave is the greatest professional I have ever met. I've never met anyone quite like him for bringing out the best in his mates.

"I don't mind where I play really as long as it's in the first team. Look at it this way. I suppose I have a preference for right-back, but I would rather play at left-half in the first team than right-back in the reserves.

"When I first made the League side it was a bit nerve-racking to play alongside so many 'greats'. But when you're with them all the time they're just ordinary blokes. Anyway you've simply got to be yourself, or you won't get anywhere, will you?"

▲ December 1970

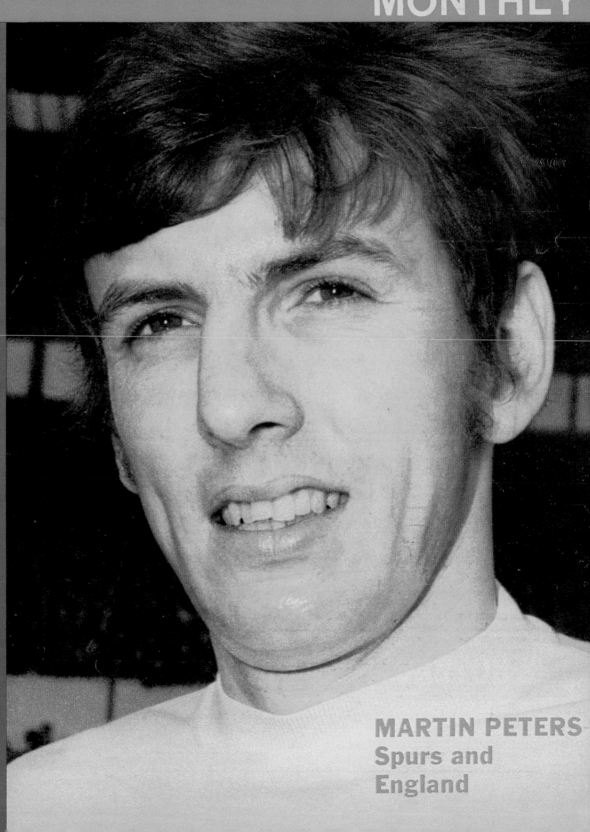

CHARLES BUCHAN'S

FOOTBALL
MONTHLY

August, 1970   Three Shillings, USA 60 cents

World Cup Special

WHERE ENGLAND WENT WRONG

Complete English and Scottish League Fixtures 1970-71

MARTIN PETERS
Spurs and England

IT WAS QPR OR WEST HAM

SO PERRYMAN WENT TO TOTTENHAM!

STEVE PERRYMAN, aged 19, goes into League Cup Final action for Tottenham unspoiled by a season of headlines and superlatives—in fact, almost apologetic about the fuss he receives . . .

Midfield dynamo Perryman, Spurs' most exciting discovery in years, is talked of as a future England international. His work-rate can be compared with that of Alan Ball and Billy Bremner and his young skills are unquestionable.

Moreover, his sense of stability and level-headed approach to the game, and his quiet, unassuming off-field manner, have endeared him to all at White Hart Lane.

Since he exploded on to the first-team scene 18 months ago no one has been slow to recognise his rich potential.

Manager Bill Nicholson says: "I'm really delighted with young Steve's progress. He's certainly come on a bundle."

Things have moved so swiftly that it would be understandable if Perryman had been overwhelmed by it all. His energy and willingness to run has upset some of the game's biggest stars.

But Perryman, amid the publicity and attention, remains shy and reserved. He talks with a refreshing honesty and mature logic that belies his tender years.

"Of course it's nice to pick up the papers and read that people are raving about you but it does not mean a lot to me. I know I have such a long way to go yet. Everything has happened so quickly I hardly know where I am," he says.

"I was thrilled just to have a regular spot in the first team. But to make Wembley as well—it's like a dream come true. I honestly didn't think I would make the first team until I was 20 or 21—if at all.

"When you consider that a player like Johnny Haynes didn't make one Cup Final appearance during his entire career you realise just how lucky you can be.

"I'm not normally the nervous type but you can bet there will be a few butterflies before this one. Still, once I'm out there I reckon I'll be O.K. In fact I can hardly wait for the big day to arrive."

That cost-nothing Perryman should make such an impact with Tottenham's hypercritical supporters reflects the lad's character and determination.

"I think it's because I always give everything for 90 minutes. I had never seen Tottenham play before I joined and I don't remember their golden era. So in a way I suppose I wasn't really conscious of the fans and just got on with the job of trying to prove my worth to the team."

Perryman, who lives with his parents and two elder brothers in a small terraced house in Nortnolt, was spotted by scout Charlie Faulkner playing for Ealing District Boys. He shrewdly decided not to sign schoolboy forms with anyone—every London club wanted his signature—until he was ready to become an apprentice professional. He trained at Tottenham but had a look at other clubs before making his choice.

"I wanted to join Queen's Park Rangers because they were the local side," recalls Perryman, "and my family wanted me to sign for West Ham, so in the end I chose Spurs!

"I didn't really know what to do. I enjoyed my football but I didn't give a thought to becoming a professional until I played for England Schoolboys.

"Then I noticed scouts at matches and it all happened from there."

Perryman went on to win four Youth caps at Spurs and spent his last year as an apprentice being guided by former England Youth manager Pat Welton.

The signs that Perryman was going to the top were already there when he made his first-team debut on the summer tour of Canada and the United States in 1969.

More than 30,000 Tottenham fans echoed that opinion when Perryman made his White Hart Lane debut against Sunderland last season.

How did Perryman feel when he stepped out to join his more renowned team-mates as a first-team player?

"Names didn't worry me. I've never really been overawed by playing with the big stars. When we play against teams like Leeds and Manchester United I sometimes think about their big names beforehand and afterwards—but not during the game.

"Skipper Alan Mullery has been a great help to me—always urging, coaxing and advising. To play alongside him and Martin Peters has been a wonderful experience. I can never repay the faith Billy Nicholson has shown in me."

Likeable Perryman, hair neatly trimmed and a snappy dresser, realises Spurs are on a hiding to nothing at Wembley.

"After the successes of Queen's Park Rangers and Swindon most people will be looking for another upset," he says. "But although we don't underestimate Villa, I can't see them stopping us."

WE WON!

There's hardly need to point it out. Big Martin Chivers, scorer of both Spurs' goals, lifts the Football League Cup on high for all to see, and there's Joe Kinnear proudly showing off the tankard that each of the Finalists received. But these pictures might so easily have been reversed. With 12 minutes of the Final to run it was the Spurs, the hot favourites, who were looking serious—and worried—about a match beginning to slip away from them. Then Chivers struck— twice, Villa had nothing further to offer after a great fight. Hence this picture . . .

Ray Bradley spotlights

PAT JENNINGS

... Spurs Super-Keeper

▲ 1971-2 Gift Book

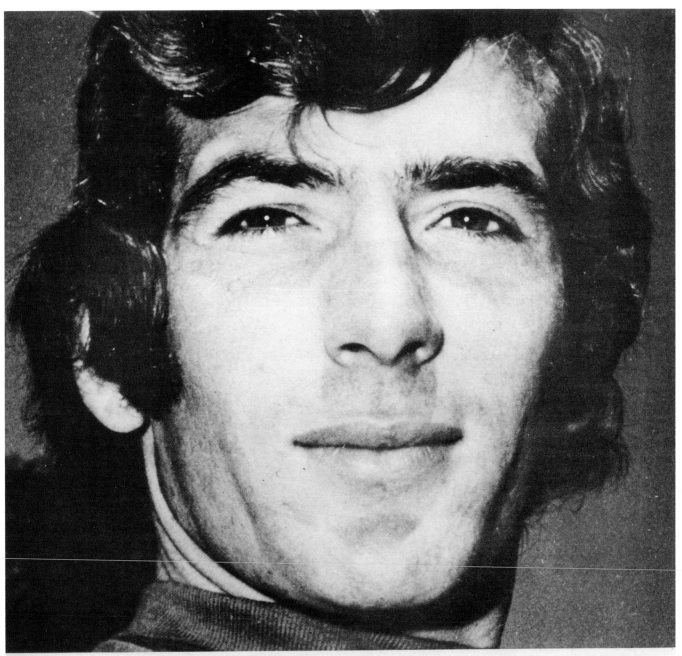

THE REMARKABLE return to top form of Spurs last season can be directly attributed to three vital factors: a collective renewal of confidence, the stirring comeback of Martin Chivers, and the sheer consistency of Irish international 'keeper Pat Jennings.

Spurs' super-keeper is that rare player . . . a man who is often breathtakingly brilliant and always utterly reliable under pressure.

Three shut-outs on Merseyside last season—two at Anfield and one at Goodison Park—are ample proof of the part Pat Jennings has played in the great Tottenham revival.

Although Spurs have shown only glimpses of their fine attacking form away from home—notably at Elland Road when they beat Leeds—there is no denying that the defence is again playing with collective determination despite the absence of Mike England for nearly a third of the season.

The fact that Big Mike was not missed unduly is a tribute to the courage and consistency of Jennings, who frequently rescued his side with a succession of brilliant displays when they were most needed—away from home.

By common consent Pat had probably his most successful season with Spurs since joining them from Watford for a mere £27,000 in 1964—a deal which represents one of the shrewdest investments ever made by manager Bill Nicholson.

On his own admission Pat claims that last season was the most pleasant he can remember in his seven-year career at White Hart Lane, even though he struggled for a period to get over a niggling injury.

" I got a knee injury against Huddersfield early in September that troubled me for quite a bit of the season," admitted Pat. " It was ligament trouble and I was out of the side for a few weeks. But when I got back into the side I was really struggling to get over it. Possibly I came back too soon but it took me a bit of time to regain my confidence.

" Luckily I've managed to steer clear of injuries in the past—serious ones I mean. I missed only one game in three seasons and had a run of 177 consecutive first-team games before injury robbed me of the chance of equalling a run of 247 successive appearances by Ted Ditchburn.

" But I can't complain. Goalkeepers come in for quite a bit of buffetting these days and I've had my share of duels with the big boys—particularly Wyn Davies—who always lets you know he's around.

" I managed to keep a high level of consistency last season. That was

Ted Ditchburn . . . a legend Jennings had to live up to

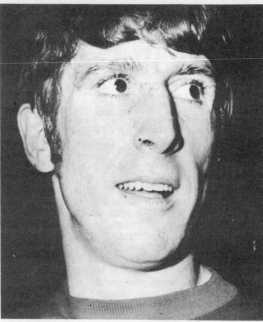

Wyn Davies . . . "lets you know he's around"

important for me because I always strive to be consistent. Goalkeepers can't afford to make mistakes, so it's no use having a blinder one week and then letting in a silly goal the next. It's important to be consistent or your form can affect the whole defence."

The courage and high level of consistency shown by Jennings last season was never better illustrated than in a memorable League Cup Final battle against Aston Villa at Wembley.

Several times in the first half his courage and coolness denied Villa the goal their aggression deserved. And again, in a delicately-balanced second-half, it was the instant reflexes of Irish india-rubber man Jennings that prevented Villa strikers Bruce Rioch and Andy Lochhead a goal, before Chivers struck with two match-winning efforts.

"That Wembley win was the highlight of the season for me," admits Jennings. "It was great to be back there again. The win was important for us because it opened the door for going back into Europe again.

"Now I'm really looking forward to playing in a big European competition again. Once you get a taste of European football it makes you hungry for more. You can't beat the sort of atmosphere you get in these games. Everyone really gets keyed up and I think the players respond to the atmosphere set by the fans."

The fans at White Hart Lane are notoriously hard to please and gave Pat a bit of stick during his early days with Spurs when he first took over from Bill Brown.

Jennings also had to fight the memories of the great Ted Ditchburn.

Pat learned to live with the legend but admits: "It was a bit rough at the time but I soon forgot it. I was only 18 when I joined Spurs from Watford and obviously it was a terrific leap for me. Perhaps I wasn't quite ready for it.

"On top of that the team was just about to break up and this caused a bit of added pressure. Obviously it took a bit of time to settle down but the fans were very good after that and really seemed to take to me.

"*Perhaps Tottenham's fans are a bit demanding. They've been fed on a rich diet of success over the years and can be a bit hard to please at first. But once they accept you they are the greatest as far as I am concerned.*"

At 26, and with 29 Irish caps to his credit ("I made my debut at 17 against Wales—it was also George Best's first game for Ireland"), Pat Jennings' stature—as a goalkeeper—is second only to Gordon Banks.

His big ambition for the future? "That's easy," says Pat, "a League championship medal. That's the greatest test of a side's ability. I've already got an F.A. Cup and League Cup winners' medal, so I'm after the hat-trick."

Pat Jennings will never admit it, but the chance of winning it may rest in his own brilliant hands.

70

MARCH 1973 20p
USA $1·20
S AFRICA 60c
NIGERIA 55k

football

MONTHLY

LEAGUE CUP FINAL

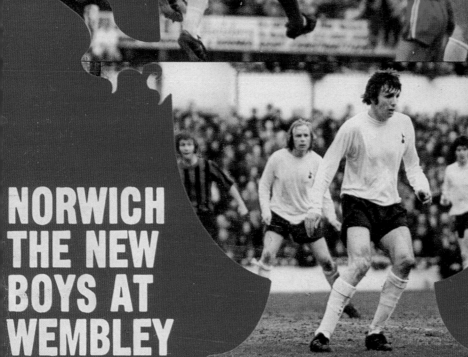

**NORWICH
THE NEW
BOYS AT
WEMBLEY**

**Tottenham
make their
fifth trip**

STEVE PERRYMAN
Spurs

The man who came back

It was a moment to savour for Spurs captain, ALAN MULLERY, as he took possession of the new UEFA Cup. His great headed goal just beat off the Wolves in the second leg at White Hart Lane . . . he was knocked unconscious in scoring it. But that's nothing to a man who only weeks earlier was on loan to Fulham, helping their relegation battle, unable to get his old Tottenham place back and right out of England consideration because of the pelvic strain which had kept him out of action for months. Then Spurs were hit by injuries and called him back. So did Sir Alf Ramsey. And then this . . .

MARTIN PETERS
Tottenham Hotspur

‘Strongest set of players in my time at White Hart Lane’

WHISPER it softly around Norwich . . . that Tottenham skipper Martin Peters feels that he has completely recaptured all his old flair and matchwinning form.

This tall, elegant midfield architect who can conjure goals when least expected, experienced a strange twist in fortunes last season. First he struggled to express his abilities, then suffered the body-blow of losing his place in the England side. But he came back in fine style to play a significant part in the UEFA Cup success over Wolves.

Says Peters: "I was substituted a few times last year and quite frankly deserved to come off. I was very disappointed at the time, but I wasn't doing my job and that is what matters. I hardly got into my stride at all until near the end of the season.

"I lost all my confidence—and that's fatal. But the important thing is not to give up, to keep plugging away in the hope that your game will suddenly click back into place.

"Even the simple things go wrong and there is no explanation for it. It just happens and you're stuck there.

"Being dropped by Sir Alf Ramsey was a big disappointment, especially after having such a long run in the side. There's still no greater feeling than when you slip on that England jersey."

What didn't help was the amount of criticism he had to endure from the fans who had previously cheered, but now jeered. That had an adverse effect on his performances. An artistic player who relies more on subtlety than strength, his style can be smothered by the hustle and bustle of the modern game.

Peters is undoubtedly the most misunderstood player in this era of "ball-winners" and "grafters." Too few realise that he is most dangerous when apparently least involved in the action.

But his qualities are fully appreciated by the men around him. The biggest boost to his confidence last season came when manager Bill Nicholson awarded him the club captaincy after Alan Mullery had been forced to rest because of a pelvic strain. He relished the extra responsibility.

"It could not have come at a better time, although we all felt very sorry for Alan," says Peters. "As skipper it made me all the more eager to do well. It's been a tremendous experience so far and the additional involvement has helped me think more about my own game.

"Despite having a rough time last season I still finished with a total of 17 goals and that by any standards isn't bad for a midfield player.

"Yet so many critics regard me as a pure striker. Nothing could be further from the truth. While I'm a creative player who is continually looking for space, I do my stint tackling and chasing in midfield and the lads would soon be on to me if I didn't.

"People point to that game against Manchester United when I scored all four goals, yet they all came as a result of me running from midfield positions."

How does Peters explain an inimitable style that Sir Alf Ramsey once described as "ten years ahead of time" and prompted Nicholson to splash £200,000 on his transfer from West Ham in March 1970?

"I think it all stems back from my early days at Upton Park," he says. "The ironic thing is that I really used to get depressed because I couldn't hold down a regular spot in the side and was shifted from one position to another. I must have played in every position for West Ham and used to have a real moan about it.

"But when I made the first-team breakthrough in midfield the experience of playing so many roles helped my game because I found I could take up so many good positions by instinct. It has just developed from there.

"I've been lucky in that my career has been associated with two clubs who rely first and foremost on skills and attacking football. And that can make a big difference to a player like myself."

Tottenham have earned a reputation as cup specialists over the years, yet they have struggled to find the endurance essential for a League challenge. Peters points to the club's burden of an overcrowded fixture list as the root cause of the problem.

"It's now getting to a stage where a club can play over 70 competitive matches in a season and still end up with nothing to show for their efforts," he says.

"It is a terrible strain on the players. Take our match against Red Star in Yugoslavia. We fought a tough match on the Wednesday afternoon, flew back straight after the game so we could have Thursday as a rest period, then we had to travel to Everton on Friday! Try working out how many miles all that lot entails.

"The way some people are talking you would think that City didn't stand a chance at Wembley.

"Norwich are a workmanlike side who never give up running and challenging for the ball. Yet they've got some really skilful players like Graham Paddon and Doug Livermore. Graham can bend a ball as good as anyone in the game and he also has a terrific shot. He is a fellow we'll have to watch very closely."

He adds, however, that Tottenham's experience of the "big" day puts them in a favourable position. "Most of us have played and won at Wembley before and remember it is only two seasons since we beat Aston Villa to take the Cup.

"The side has changed only slightly since then with youngsters like Ray Evans, Terry Naylor and John Pratt emerging with great success. *One big advantage is that Martin Chivers has regained his goal-scoring touch after a depressing start.* Last season he scored so many goals that he was bound to suffer some reaction sooner or later.

"Then there is Alan Gilzean who is a great asset to the side. Yet at times he's infuriating. One minute he'll try something that doesn't come off then the next he's popped one in the back of the net!

"One player who very rarely gets a mention is Cyril Knowles. He has been a revelation this season and if there is a better attacking full-back in the country then I'd like to meet him.

"This is the strongest set of players in my time at White Hart Lane."

One part Peters is slow to discuss is his own. "I've been more than happy with my form," he says, "the goals have been coming and I feel I am playing some of the best football of my career. But it's not hard with so many good players around you.

"We are all looking forward to the match and I'd like to play an important part in the result." *Point taken, Norwich?*

▲ March 1973 | August 1973 ▶

FAMILY ALBUM

Another master move by Tottenham and England ace Martin Peters—this time on the chess board—watched by his wife Kathy and their smiling children, Lee-Ann and Grant

MANCHESTER CITY chief Malcom Allison calls him "the finest centre-forward in Britain." Leeds United manager Don Revie describes him as "the most powerful and improved player in League Soccer."

The man they are talking about is Tottenham's explosive heavyweight striker Martin Chivers, a player who is admired by colleague and opponent alike.

Long and leggy, Chivers epitomises all that is good in English football. Standing 6ft. 2in. and weighing nearly 13½ stone, his massive, superbly proportional frame—enabling him to shrug off vigorous physical challenges—coupled with his powerful shooting and knack of seizing the half-chance make him the most complete forward in the game today.

His ambling stride makes him look lazy and he is deceptive both in turn of speed and mastery of the ball.

The success story of Chivers is vintage boys' magazine material. Signed in January 1968 from Southampton for a then record fee of £125,000, the holder of a record 17 England Under-23 caps, he opened his career with Spurs by scoring the winner on his debut against Sheffield Wednesday at Hillsborough.

Then tragedy took over. In September 1968 the man Bill

TRUE GRIT!

MARTIN CHIVERS SPURS

▲ December 1971

olson had bought to try to g back the glory, glory days Tottenham was carried off n White Hart Lane after an cuous-looking tackle with st's Bob McKinlay.

e was rushed to the Royal onal Orthopaedic Hospital, more, for an emergency ation on severed ligaments is left knee. A hospital bul- described the injury as "one he worst of its kind in the ital's history."

his cruel blow came at a time n Chivers looked like justify- every penny of the huge fee olson had spent on him.

ays Chivers: "It's a bit of a tery just how I damaged the . There was no physical con- I just fell awkwardly. It 't really dawn upon me just serious the injury was until next morning in hospital.

t was murder lying there the knowledge that I ldn't be able to kick a ball six months. My leg was sed in plaster from foot to h. The heartbreaking thing that I was really settling n to play some good foot-"

all, Chivers was lost to the e for nearly a year. The back to fitness was long and ful and on top of that nag- fears remained as to whether ould play again.

t 22, Britain's most expensive and a player who had been narked by Sir Alf Ramsey as ossible for the 1970 World in Mexico faced the Soccer pheap.

hivers takes up the story: "So y people were prepared to e me off that I began to des- myself of ever playing again. But I was determined to get . I sweated for months with ndbag straddled across my leg which I had to lift up down over 100 times a day. here I must pay tribute to wife and the surgeon, Mr. ky, who continually urged on."

fter what had seemed a life- , Chivers made his first pub- ppearance against St. Albans for Spurs' reserve side in 1969.

he knee passed the test, but as not until the end of the that he returned to the first . He was dropped, substi- d with alarming regularity, lved in transfer speculation, then recalled permanently to first team.

uddenly and sensationally all grit and determination re-

turned. From a £125,000 has-been, Chivers rocketed back to fame with some scintillating performances which delighted his one-time hyper-critical White Hart Lane regulars.

No player did more than the muscular Chivers to help Spurs lift the League Cup at Wembley last season. And after slamming two match-winning efforts past Aston Villa goalkeeper John Dunn, his manager, Bill Nicholson, jubilantly exclaimed: "I don't like to single out players for special praise, but I thought Martin's display was absolutely magnificent."

Praise indeed from a manager given to weighing his every word.

And it didn't stop there. After topping the Tottenham goalscorers' list with 21 League goals out of a meagre overall return of 54 he earned England recognition from Sir Alf Ramsey. In five internationals he averaged a

Chivers being carried off at Tottenham in September, 1968

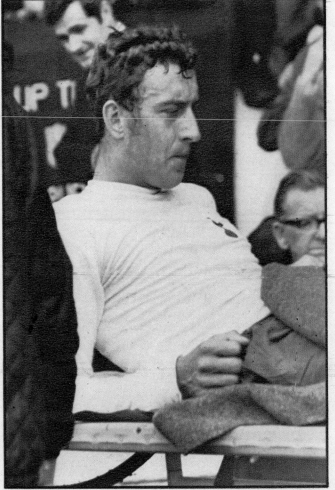

goal a game, including two brilliant efforts in an emphatic 3-1 victory over Scotland at Wembley in May.

How does he explain the blossoming of his career? "Confidence," he replies. "I now know that I can take an opponent on. I know I can hold my own in the top class. The widening of my game is a natural result and comes with belief in my ability.

"It has made me feel that I can do more and varied tasks which once seemed beyond me. Above all I am now using my height to the best possible advantage.

"People have apparently been baffled by my success. Certainly nobody has been more grateful than myself. I would have settled for a regular place at Spurs, let alone an England chance.

"I've always believed I could do well given a fair chance. But obviously the injury I got

stopped me in my tracks. Then once I was fit I found it hard to get back into the groove of things.

"Let's face it, if a golfer didn't pick up his clubs for a year would he be able to find his swing immediately?" The biggest boost to Chivers' confidence came when he survived that startling shake-up after Spurs' inglorious exit from the F.A. Cup at the hands of struggling London neighbours Crystal Palace two seasons ago.

Among the victims of Bill Nicholson's purge then were established internationals Jimmy Greaves, Alan Gilzean, Cyril Knowles and Joe Kinnear. That Chivers remained reflected the club's appreciation of his effort and determination.

Chivers, son of a Southampton docker, started his working life painting houses.

In September 1962 he was playing in the Southampton Senior League in Rownham's Park before a handful of spectators. Within weeks—and on his 17th birthday—he signed as a professional with the Saints and two days later was thrown into the first team against Charlton at The Dell.

A yearning for success with a more fashionable club prompted him into asking for a move after a hatful of goals had made him one of the hottest properties on the Hampshire club's books.

Says Chivers: "I spent six happy years at Southampton. The club was good to me and the fans treated me wonderfully well. You couldn't wish for a friendlier bunch.

"But I was ambitious and the time came for me to look to the future.

"Yet events at Tottenham made me feel as if I'd taken a wrong decision. But all that is behind me now.

"People have been kind enough to rate me a certainty for the World Cup in 1974. That's not for me to decide. Of course I'd dearly love to play for England again this season.

"But above all I want more success with Spurs. That League Cup triumph has whetted my appetite for a quick return to Wembley. Those two goals were easily the finest moments of my career.

"Everyone was so patient and understanding during my long lay-off that I feel I owe it to them to score as many goals as possible to repay their faith and make up for lost time."

FOR the second year running a goalkeeper was accorded the honour of being named Footballer of the Year by the Football Writers' Association.

Last season Gordon Banks received the award and following in his footsteps comes Tottenham's big, amiable Irishman Pat Jennings.

Possessing the largest pair of hands in Soccer, Jennings' goalkeeping can be summed up in one word—FLAWLESS! His sheer consistency, lightning reflexes and positive handling has singled him out as the undisputed World's No. I

A placid, unassuming character, he gave one of the finest exhibitions of keeping for many years in Spurs' I–I draw at Anfield last season when he saved TWO penalties.

On the left you can see him diving to stop the second from Liverpool skipper Tommy Smith.

PAT JENNINGS – Footballe

" How do you get past this fellow?" That seems the reaction from Arsenal's Alan Ball

A rare sight . . . Jennings beaten at White Hart Lane by Kevin Keegan

Feet first to stop Don Rogers

▲ 1973–4 Gift Book

f the Year and World's No. 1 keeper

A powerful right-hander clears his lines against Derby

Safe as houses as
he collects this Norwich
cross in the League Cup Final

Postscript

It says everything for the Spurs tradition of style and innovation that just one team, Arthur Rowe's 'push and run' side of the early 1950s, produced two of this country's greatest managers.

No one needs reminding what became of Alf Ramsey. After ending his playing career at Tottenham in May 1955 he steered unfashionable Ipswich from the Third Division to the League title in just seven years, followed by masterminding the ultimate prize with England in 1966. Knighted soon after, Sir Alf's England performed creditably at the following World Cup in Mexico in 1970, but, as was the case with his mentor Arthur Rowe, he stayed too loyal to the old guard, and was eventually sacked for failing to take England to the 1974 World Cup. Sir Alf died from Alzheimer's disease in his adopted Ipswich in April 1999, aged 79.

In the same month that Ramsey left White Hart Lane to begin his managerial life, May 1955, his fellow defender Bill Nicholson went straight from the dressing room onto the club's coaching staff.

When his Tottenham side did the Double in 1961 Nicholson became one of only four men to win a championship medal as a player and manager with the same team.

From then on the name Bill Nicholson remained synonymous with Tottenham. Even when he resigned in 1974, he was so loved by his players that several begged him to change his mind. As it happened, his retirement from football lasted less than a year and, from Spurs, only a little longer.

After working as a scout for West Ham, Nicholson was asked by Keith Burkinshaw, one of his successors as manager, to come back as a consultant. This he did for a further 21 years before finally retiring in 1997 at the age of 78. He remained Club President however.

Although he never gained the knighthood that many felt was his due, Nicholson was made an OBE in 1975, a Freeman of the Borough of Haringey in 1998, and in 1999 was further honoured when the short road that leads from Tottenham High Road to the main entrance of White Hart Lane was renamed Bill Nicholson Way.

Almost to the end of his life, Nicholson and his wife Grace, better known as 'Darkie' (her sister was Fairy), remained in the modest semi-detached house they had occupied in Creighton Road since the 1950s, a short distance from the ground. (Darkie herself was a much-loved presence around the club, except on match days, when Nicholson banned her, and their two daughters, from attending.)

'Billy Nick', as he was widely known, died in October 2004 at the age of 85. Two weeks later a crowd of 10,000 attended a memorial service for him at White Hart Lane, many of whom were born long after his glory years as manager.

Returning to 1955, Nicholson had joined the coaching staff in the same month that manager Arthur Rowe had stepped down.

After recovering his health, Rowe reappeared two years later, first as a coach at West Bromwich Albion, then as manager at Crystal Palace, whom he led to promotion from the Fourth Division, in the same season as Tottenham's Double.

Yet again his health deteriorated however, so he resigned in 1966, only to pop up later in various roles at Palace, Orient and Millwall. Despite his health problems, Rowe was 87 when he died in 1993.

In addition to Ramsey and Nicholson, several of Rowe's other players also went into management.

Ron Burgess left Spurs in 1954 to play for Swansea Town. After becoming their player-manager a year later, he was responsible for persuading a young Cliff Jones to join Tottenham rather than Arsenal.

Another of the starlets Burgess pointed towards Spurs was Pat Jennings, his goalkeeper at Watford during a four year stint as manager from 1959-63. This was followed by two seasons at non-League Hendon, whom he took to the Amateur Cup Final in 1965.

After this he worked as a stock controller for a stationery company, and finally as a warehouseman, before retiring to South Wales. He died in 2005, aged 87.

Giant centre-half Harry Clarke also became a player-manager, at Llanelli, after which he managed Southern League Romford. Clarke later worked for a security transit company in Ilford and died in 2000, aged 77.

After leaving Spurs in 1956, Eddie Baily played for Port Vale, Nottingham Forest and Leyton Orient, where he became a coach in 1961. He then joined his former team-mate Bill Nicholson's coaching staff at White Hart Lane, becoming assistant manager after the death of Harry Evans. Baily later worked as a scout for Chelsea and West Ham before retirement. For a while he also taught PE in an Enfield School.

George Robb meanwhile continued the teaching career he had kept up during his years at Tottenham. At that time he taught at Christ's College, Finchley, but after hanging up his boots he joined the staff at Ardingly College, where he remained until his retirement in 1986. Robb still lives near the College, in West Sussex.

Tommy Harmer's career at Spurs faltered after the signing of John White, and in October 1960 he was sold to Watford for £6,000. From there he moved to Tommy Docherty's Chelsea, making only a handful of appearances as the Blues made a speedy return to the top division. Most memorably, in February 1964, a day before his 36th birthday, the Hackney born 'Harmer the Charmer' engineered the two goals that sank Spurs at White Hart Lane.

Thereafter he coached at Chelsea before leaving the game in 1967. He later worked as a bank messenger, and died, aged 79, on Christmas Day, 2007.

Len Duquemin made his last League appearance for Tottenham in the 1956-57 season, subsequently spending four seasons in non-League. He finally left the game in 1962 to run a newsagent's, close to White Hart Lane, then became a publican in Cheshunt, close to the club's training ground. He died in 2003, aged 78.

Like Duquemin Ted Ditchburn also ran a newsagent's near White Hart Lane, a business he started while still a player. After his last appearance for Spurs in 1958 he then spent six years at non-League Romford, where he opened a sports shop. He died 2005, aged 84.

As for trainer Cecil Poynton, he kept this role until 1972, becoming physio until he retired in 1975. He died in 1983, aged 81.

And what of the mercurial Irishman, Danny Blanchflower?

Aged 38 when he finally hung up his boots in 1964, Blanchflower moved straight into journalism, first with *The Observer*, then with the *Sunday Express*. In 1967 he also worked as a TV commentator in the USA. That he insisted on being openly blunt about the lacklustre fare on offer, rather than hype it up as his paymasters wished, soon led to a parting of the ways.

After this Blanchflower severed his connections with football, until persuaded back as manager of Northern Ireland. He lasted two seasons, from 1976-78, followed by barely nine, unhappy months in the hotseat at Stamford Bridge.

Having tried management he was then relieved to resume work as an acerbic newspaper columnist.

Later struck down by Alzheimer's disease, Blanchflower died in 1993, aged 67. He is commemorated by the Danny Blanchflower Playing Fields in East Belfast.

Terry Medwin's playing career ended when he broke a leg during a pre-season tour of South Africa in 1963. Thereafter he coached at Fulham before joining his first club, Swansea, as assistant to John Toshack. He still lives in Wales. Martin Peters, awarded an MBE for his services to the game, enjoyed six seasons with Norwich after leaving Spurs, had a final year as player-manager with Sheffield United, then a successful second career in insurance. Since retiring he has worked as a matchday host at White Hart Lane.

Of his team-mates from the Double era, Dave Mackay joined Brian Clough's struggling Derby County in 1968, then led them as captain to the Second Division title. The one member of the Double side to make an impact in management, his first job was with Swindon in 1971 as player-manager. He then took over Nottingham Forest before returning to manage Derby in the wake of Brian Clough's resignation.

Unpopular though he was at the start (as anyone would have been following 'Ol' Bighead'), Mackay emulated Clough by steering the Rams to their second League title, in 1975. A year later he was sacked, after which he had spells with Walsall, in the Middle East, Doncaster and Birmingham.

Cliff Jones was the last Double winner to play in Spurs' first team, finally leaving for Fulham in October 1968 at the age of 33. In 1972 he became PE teacher at Highbury Grove School. More recently Jones has worked as a match day host at White Hart Lane, as has Phil Beal.

Ron Henry went on to run a market garden from his home in Hertfordshire, but carried on assisting the Spurs youth team on matchdays until 2006. He thereby served the club for nearly 52 years.

Peter Baker left White Hart Lane in 1965 to manage Durban City in South Africa, and stayed on to build a furniture business. Since then he has returned to the Enfield area.

Bobby Smith was transferred to Brighton in 1964, but after only one season became a decorator. He also later drove a mini-cab.

Les Allen enjoyed a more illustrious swansong, having three high scoring years at up-and-coming QPR, who had paid Spurs a record fee of £21,000.

After retiring in 1969 he then had a season as QPR manager, followed by two years at Swindon. Subsequently he became a model-maker for an Essex company, but stayed in close touch with the game

as the father of one-time Spurs striker Clive, and QPR and Charlton player Bradley, who eventually became a youth coach at Spurs.

Like Cliff Jones, Terry Dyson left Spurs for Fulham, in 1965. From there he went to Colchester and non-League Guildford, before managing non-League Dagenham and Borehamwood. Also like Jones he taught PE in London schools. Dyson now works part-time as an assessor of schoolboys for the FA.

Maurice Norman played on until a severe leg break in a Spurs friendly in November 1965 ended his career, thereby clearing the way for Jack Charlton to secure his place in Alf Ramsey's England team for the World Cup. Norman then opened a wool shop in Frinton in Essex, but when that business collapsed, returned to his beloved East Anglia to work as a gardener.

Goalkeeper Bill Brown, who made way for Pat Jennings in 1966, ended his playing career in Canada with Toronto Falcons. He settled there to work as a property developer and joined the Ontario government's Land Department in 1975 before retiring to live in the province in 1995. He died in 2004.

Tony Marchi rejoined Spurs from Italy to replace the injured Dave Mackay in the European Cup Winners' Cup final in Rotterdam in 1963. He then left Spurs a second time in 1965 and had spells as player-manager with non-League Cambridge City and as manager of Northampton, before quitting the game to run a DIY shop in Essex.

Frank Saul, just 18 when he played against Feyenoord in the European Cup in 1962, did not fulfil his early promise, though he scored in the 1967 FA Cup Final against Chelsea. He left for Southampton in 1968 – a makeweight in the deal that brought Martin Chivers to White Hart Lane – ending his career at QPR and Millwall.

After he left Spurs, Jimmy Greaves had a season at West

Ham, then several years in non-League football in the London area. For Barnet, then in the Southern League, he managed 25 goals in one season, quite something for a heavy drinking 38 year old.

But Greaves conquered his habit and went on to a successful second career as one half of the 'Saint and Greavesie' television double act, working alongside the former Liverpool striker, Ian St John.

Now he entertains around the south-east with his after-dinner speaking and theatre appearances, reminiscing about the old days with the likes of Ron 'Chopper' Harris and Pat Jennings. He is also the author of several books.

Greaves' strike partner Alan Gilzean was said to have had no interest in football at all after he left Spurs in 1974, and according to one source ended up managing a haulage company in Enfield, before retiring to Weston-super-Mare.

Pat Jennings, meanwhile, was famously transferred to Arsenal in 1977, the Spurs management assuming that he was by then near the end of his career. Jennings of course played a further eight years for the Gunners, before returning to Tottenham for a farewell season in the second team, thereby staying fit enough to feature for Northern Ireland in the 1986 World Cup. He now works as a goalkeeping coach for Spurs and lives in Hertfordshire.

Mike England and Alan Mullery both enjoyed success in management, England as manager of Wales, Mullery with Brighton, whom he led from the Third to the First Division, developing along the way such players as Mark Lawrenson, John Gregory, Gary Stevens and Michael Robinson. He then went on to Charlton, Crystal Palace and QPR, before ending his managerial career back at Brighton. He is now a successful speaker and media pundit.

Joe Kinnear also went into management, although not before

ending his playing career at Brighton and Wimbledon. Under his management the Dons achieved a sixth place finish in the Premier League in 1993-94, despite ground-sharing with Crystal Palace. Kinnear also took the club to FA Cup and League Cup semi-finals in 1997 before suffering a heart attack in 1999 and standing down. He returned to management with Luton Town and then Nottingham Forest, saving them from relegation before resigning in 2004.

Cyril Knowles, who inspired the celebrated ditty, 'Nice one Cyril' before Spurs' 1973 League Cup final, retired as a player in 1976. He went on to become assistant manager at Middlesbrough, then manager at Darlington, Torquay and Hartlepool, where he was still working when struck down by cancer in 1991, at the age of 47. A stand at the club's Victoria Park was later named in his memory.

Steve Perryman, who eventually notched up a club record of 854 appearances, moved to Oxford and then to Brentford as player-manager before retiring in 1990. Having coached abroad, he is currently a director of Exeter City and runs a sports and travel business.

And finally we come to White Hart Lane itself, backdrop to so many *Football Monthly* pictures.

Since 1980 the old familiar ground has been completely rebuilt on three sides, with only the main entrance on Tottenham High Road and the East Stand still just about recognisable from the street outside. And yet through all Spurs' travails since the glory years, and for all the modern stands and banks of seats, it remains just as it was when *Football Monthly* was a regular visitor; a beating heart in the centre of a north London suburb whose name is known to millions around the world.

All thanks to the Spurs, and to the men on these pages who brought such glory to its High Road.

Index

Further reading

Blanchflower, Danny *The Double and Before* Nicholas Kaye (1962)
Bowler, David *Danny Blanchflower: The Biography of a Visionary* Orion (1997)
Bowler, David *Winning Isn't Everything: the Biography of Alf Ramsey* Gollancz (1999)
Brown, Deryk *Tottenham Hotspur Story* Arthur Barker (1971)
Burgess, Ron *Football – My Life* Souvenir Press (1952)
Davies, Hunter *The Glory Game – a Year in the Life of Tottenham Hotspur* Weidenfeld & Nicholson *(1972)* plus numerous reprints
Ferris, Ken *The Double: The Inside Story of Spurs' Triumphant 1960-61 Season* Mainstream (1999)
Finn, Ralph *Spurs Again – The Story of the League Cup Season 1970-71* Robert Hale (1971)
Finn, Ralph *Spurs Go Marching On* Soccer Book Club (1964)
Finn, Ralph *Spurs Supreme – a Review of Soccer's Greatest Ever Side in 1960-61* Robert Hale (1961)
Finn, Ralph *The Official History of Tottenham Hotspur FC 1882-1972* Robert Hale (1972)
Greaves, Jimmy *It's a Funny Old Life* Arthur Barker (1990)
Greaves, Jimmy *This One's On Me* Arthur Barker (1979)
Hale, Steve *Mr Tottenham Hotspur: Bill Nicholson OBE – Memories of a Spurs Legend* Football World (2005)
Holland, Julian *Spurs – A History of Tottenham Hotspur Football Club* Sportsman Book Club (1957)
Holland, Julian *The Double* Heinemann (1961)
Inglis, Simon (ed) *The Best of Charles Buchan's Football Monthly* English Heritage (2006)
Jennings, Pat *Pat Jennings – an Autobiography* Willow Books (1983)
Kinnear, Joe and Davies, Hunter *Joe Kinnear – Still Crazy* Andre Deutsch (2000)
Mackay, Dave and Knight, Martin *The Real Mackay: The Dave Mackay Story* Mainstream (2005)
McKinstry, Leo *Sir Alf: A Major Reappraisal of the Life and Times of England's Greatest Football Manager* HarperSport (2007)
Marquis, Max *Anatomy of a Football Manager – Sir Alf Ramsey* Sportsman Book Club (1972)
Mullery, Alan *Alan Mullery – the Autobiography* Headline (2007)
Mullery, Alan *In Defence of Spurs* Sportsman Book Club (1970)
Mullery, Alan and Trevillion, Paul *Double Bill: The Bill Nicholson Story* Mainstream (2005)
Nicholson, Bill *Glory Glory: My Life with Spurs* Macmillan (1984)
Perryman, Steve *A Man for All Seasons – an Autobiography* Arthur Barker (1985)
Peters, Martin *The Ghost of '66: the Autobiography* Orion (2006)
Ponting, Ivan and Morgan, Tom *Tottenham Hotspur: Player by Player* Know the Score Books (2008)
Soar, Phil *And the Spurs Go Marching On – The First Hundred Years* Hamlyn (1982)
Soar, Phil *Tottenham Hotspur History* Mitchell Beazley (1995)

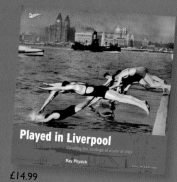
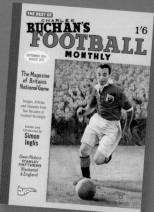
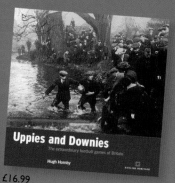

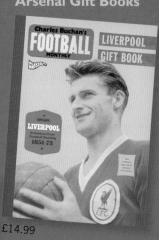

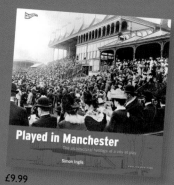

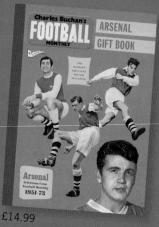